Revelation ---at last

Richard W. Turner, Sr.

COROIN BOOKS

Published by Coroin Books
https://coroin.com/books

ISBNs
eBook (EPUB): 978-1-963770-09-4
Paperback: 978-1-963770-10-0
Hardcover: 978-1-963770-11-7
LCCN (Library of Congress Control Number): 2025944135

Cover illustration by Carlos Maraver
https://vectorlance.com

REVELATION ---at last

Revelation ---at last is a continuation of some of my experiences as a boy, a military pilot, a family man, and parts of my life up to the present. As in my first book, *Third Chance*, these are short stories that were written for the edification of my children and, hopefully, whatever family that follows me.

The stories are not in chronological order. They have not been exaggerated. If anything, I have tried to keep them short enough that the reader will not get bored. But they are all true stories, and I am responsible for their accuracy.

With this in mind, I must give thanks to my three children: Sharyn Elizabeth Turner Larson of Plano, Texas, Richard (Rick) W., Jr. Turner of Fort Mill, South Carolina, and Nancy Lynn Turner Blaylock of West Richland, Washington.

This writing is dedicated to their patience, understanding of my efforts, and the many times their presence and their own memories have triggered some of the details and the accuracy of these stories.

We often are so proud of our children. But as I have written these and other stories, I realize that Caroline and I have been truly blessed with children that we have not only loved, but also honestly liked as people.

Caroline has not been with me physically as I have put this book together. As you read this book, you will know the reason why. But her sweet spirit, loving guidance, and correcting direction have been manifested through our three children as they watched and helped me in the whole effort.

Thank you, Kids. This is all dedicated to you and your love.
I love you, always. Daddy.

FORWARD

We're releasing this book on my grandparents' 81st wedding anniversary this October. Their story started a few months earlier. Here's how my grandfather remembers the night they first met:

> Saturday, August 26, [I went to] the home of my blind date.
> At first sight, I immediately fell in love with the 103-pound
> brunette dressed in her basic black dress and high heels.
> Her name was Caroline.

It was only a few months after we published his first book, *Third Chance*, that my grandmother was hospitalized and then passed on. Most, if not all, of the words in this second book were written from a place of grief and loss.

I appreciate how raw and real my grandfather is, sharing openly the pain and sadness he is walking through: the loneliness, the emptiness, the sorrow after losing his wife of 56 years. And his stories from back in the day are from a time so long ago that it almost reads like fiction. Our modern world seems so disposable and consumable compared to that other time.

Changes from the first edition include punctuation, minor grammatical adjustments for readability, a few footnotes for context, and one editorial change moving the chapter *Revelation ---at last* to the penultimate position, preceding the sign off in *Thank You, Dear Reader*.

I'm grateful for the continued collaboration with the amazing and talented Carlos Maraver (vectorlance.com), whose masterful attention to detail and brilliant continuation of the stained-glass motif used for the first book will be carried across the entire collection.

In the *Dedication*, my grandfather says this book was written for his children and "whatever family that follows me". This second edition exists thanks to the efforts of some of those "followers", including his great-granddaughters Ashlin Larson and Madailein Larson. <3

It probably goes without saying that I am here today because the story that began one Saturday in August 1944 continued.

The next afternoon, Sunday, we took in a movie.
The theme song was *Always* by Irving Berlin.
After calls on Monday and Tuesday, we dated
Wednesday night and every night thereafter.
After three weeks, I asked Caroline to marry me.
She said we had not known each other long enough.
I waited 10 more days.
On September 29, I gave her a diamond ring. She accepted.
On October 8, 1944, Caroline and I committed ourselves
to each other in marriage.
Naturally, the organist played *Always*.

May this book be remembered as one man's confident testimony to the covenant of undying love, faithfully kept, without end. Always.

Erik R. Larson
Galveston, Texas
October 8, 2025

Acknowledgements

With Thanks

I T TAKES MANY HOURS and much effort to get beyond the mere writing of stories, much less compiling and putting a story or stories into the form of a book.

It was bad enough to try to learn how to use a computer at age 78, and then use the "hunt-and-peck" method of typing.

Fortunately, I have a son who continually "cleaned" my hard drive and rescued partial stories that seemed to "disappear." Thank you, Rick. And thanks to Diane, your wife, for her patience as you spent time here on those rescue missions.

Each of my daughters reminded me of things their younger minds remember, and we tend to forget as we age. Sharyn and Nancy, both of you, along with your sister-in-love Diane, have done so much to help this emotional cripple try to get through this hardest time of my life. Each of you has shared your faith that my Caroline is now with Jesus. Thanks to each of you.

Of course, my love and thanks go out to each of the families of in-laws, and grandchildren, and great-grandchildren.

All of this has contributed to easing these last steps of putting together this book. But perhaps the last steps need the most acknowledgement: The formatting, paging, etc.

Thank you, Grandson Erik Richard Larson and friend Jason M. Schlitz, for your hard work and effort. You are the computer gurus who know how to do that sort of thing. You did it with THIRD CHANCE, and now with REVELATION ---at last. If this book has any success, I must give you great words of thanks. So I will: Thank you, Erik and Jason.

How can I ever thank my Favorite Editor (I mean, favorite editor) — my daughter, Sharyn Turner Larson. Sharyn spent hours and hours cleaning up the "gramer" and "spleling errors" (which I always accepted), and suggesting revisions of sentences and thoughts (which I didn't always accept). Most always, she made the stories more readable. For this, I again can only say — with my most fatherly and heartfelt love — THANKS, Sharyn.

CONTENTS

INTRODUCTION

THIS IS THE SECOND time that I have been presumptuous enough to try to "write a book." It just doesn't seem that an ordinary person like myself would have anything to offer to anyone else. Yet, I feel compelled to put these words in this book as a way of sharing an insight into the events, influences, culture, mores, and some historical facts of the times in which I was raised, and the results of all of this. I am 78 years of age. I was born March 14, 1924. The Lord is so good to give me this number of years.

As of this writing, this computer is more understanding, trying to get along with me, than I am having the patience to get along with such a modern marvel. I have finished all of the stories for this book. If I try to resurrect any more stories of my life at this time, I may be guilty of telling lies.

My mind is tired, and, because it is now over one year since the hardest day of my life, I need to try to put closure to this re-living and telling of stories of the past — stories that, even now, still hurt to re-tell. I am trying to get through all of the past year, but I will never, nor do I wish to ever, get over these events. I need to get THROUGH them.

If you are reading these words, you are a part of my grieving and healing process. You will come to understand this as you read this book.

If other events in my life should come to my mind and memory, perhaps there will be another book that follows *Third Chance* and now, *Revelation ---at last.*

LOOPING A C-46

THE C-46 AIRPLANE WAS built by the Curtis Aircraft Co. for the transport of troops and cargo. It was the largest cargo aircraft used during World War II. The wingspan was 108' and it measured 76'4" from nose to tail. The pilots sat 15' high in the cockpit. The plane was powered by two Pratt & Whitney engines that generated 2000 horsepower each. There were two cargo bays, one upper and one lower. Although small by today's standards, the C-46 was a very large airplane, used to some extent in other theaters of the war, but specifically in the CBI, or the China-Burma-India Theater of World War II.

This is the airplane that was used to establish the first-ever full-scale airlift of military supplies. The routes of this airlift were from the Assam Valley, in what was northeast India, to supply depots in China. The Assam Valley was covered by tea plantations, but some areas of tea were replaced by stone and then later asphalt runways during World War II. The airplanes were loaded in India and flown over the Himalayan Mountains to bases in China, offloaded, and returned to the bases in India. The routes were over mountains that were higher in several places than the airplanes could fly.

We had none of the sophisticated weather prediction equipment of today, so the airplane had to be constructed strong enough to be able to fly through some of the worst weather on this planet. There were monsoon rains, ice, hail the size of grapefruit, horrific winds, and storms with tremendous updrafts and downdrafts that caused the airplane to lose 500 feet or more when you flew into them. We could not fly over them, and we had no way of locating them, so we just had to — fly. This meant we had to rely on elementary navigation calculations, radio beams, and some parts of your anatomy. This translates into a magnetic compass, earphones, your head, and the seat of your pants.

Sometimes the winds would blow you off-course, or your radio didn't work, or lots of things could go wrong. Because of these conditions, you and your crew became candidates to join your fallen buddies on what we affectionately called the mountains of that area: The Hump. Or the Aluminum Trail, so called because so many planes crashed on the mountains. These are the only aluminum-clad mountains in the world.

Why do I tell you about all of these things?

Because I want you to know about the C-46: its strengths, power, and the trust we had to put into its capabilities to do the work it was designed to do. Many of us wondered if this great airplane could do one more thing: an inside loop! Of course, there was only one way to find out.

The military establishment would never allow such an unnecessary maneuver, but some pilots NEEDED to know all about the airplanes they were flying. And pilots aren't stupid. A little crazy, perhaps, but always very careful! So the time came when the temptation was too great to ignore.

We had heard of a pilot who had tried to slow-roll a B-17 bomber. He did not complete the roll, but he bent a lot of parts of the airplane. When he landed, he was told how much it would cost to repair the B-17. It would cost a small fortune, so he was promoted to a One Star General, and the money was deducted from his pay until the cost of repairs was satisfied. I am not sure if the story was true or not. Perhaps the only truth is that we had, indeed, heard the story.

Problems happen with mechanical things, and when they are repaired, it is prudent to test the results. This is especially true of airplanes. (See, we pilots aren't stupid.) One day, it fell to our lot to test some repairs on one of our C-46s. This meant no load of cargo — just a couple of pilots, a crew chief, and a radio operator. We were all of one mind: let's try to loop a C-46.

The C-46 had a top speed, loaded, of about 180 mph. This wasn't fast enough to outrun the Japanese fighters, but then, they wouldn't fly under the conditions we did anyway. Well, most of the time. There were times, however, when it was clear enough for them to harass us, and when we saw them, we hoped for some of those clouds and storms.

Back to the story.

When we finished all of the required tests, we sort of let ourselves drift away from our base. We needed two things. First, we needed to get away from any military field where prying eyes may not appreciate what we were sacrificing ourselves to prove. Second, we needed to get as much air beneath our plane as possible so that we had some chance of being able to dive and pick up enough speed to, hopefully, accomplish the loop.

We nosed over our airplane and started our shallow dive. This increased our speed to over 170 mph. We needed more speed, so we nosed over some more. Now we were up to about 185 mph. Would the wings stay on? Then a little more nudge gave us just under 200 mph.

And the wings were still there.

Now would come the test. We pulled back on the yoke and started into our upward part of the loop.

Any airplane needs to have thrust to give it speed. Then it needs lift to keep it from stalling. The combination makes these huge machines, made of metal, fly. But if you take away the thrust, or power, you decrease the amount of airflow around the wings. This creates a condition called stalling. That is not a good condition to be in when you are flying. There is nothing left to hold you up. If you do not immediately either get enough power to correct the situation or get your nose down to increase the lift on the wings, you will stall. And if you are not skilled enough to prevent it, you probably will go into a spin. Either condition is not only uncomfortable, but it is rather deadly. That is why we needed the altitude and the speed.

Up we went, throttles at full power, screaming into the wild blue yonder. We would be the first to loop a C-46!!!

Upward we flew. Then the airspeed indicator started to come back down below 190 mph. That is when we felt the first slight tremble throughout the airplane. Suddenly, the airspeed was down to 175 mph. We tried to give the engines more throttle, but they were already at maximum settings. Now the airspeed was approaching 150 mph, and the trembling indicated we were about to stall, because the attitude of the airplane was such that we had lost most of the lift on the wings.

We had started our loop at about 16,000 ft. and our descent had carried us to about 14,000 ft. As we started up the loop, we had returned to a little less than our original altitude. But that was all this C-46 was going to let us do. It really shook as it fell into a full-fledged stall, but we were able to keep it from falling off to either side into a spin. Perhaps because of its size, it remained stable as we stalled straight ahead. We had plenty of altitude to recover our airspeed, and we even throttled back on those trusty engines as we regained control of our airplane.

The mighty Curtis Commando C-46 could not be looped after all.

Needless to say, we did not wear the Stars of a General on our shoulders either.

A Basement Playground

I T IS FUN TO recall some of the favorite childhood events and the places where they took place. Let me share some of my memories with you. Some took place while I was a child, and some of them are from times as I grew into being a youth and even into adulthood.

From the age of four, our family of five lived at 101 Hill Avenue, Johnson City, NY. My dad, Henry W. Turner, my mother, M. Ethel (Kreidler, spelled correctly), my older brother Henry (Hank), Jr., my younger brother Roger, and myself. Our home was a two-story house with a cellar, sometimes called a basement.

This cellar contained the washing machine with a manual wringer that Hank got his arm caught in (no permanent damage), a pair of cement tubs for something that mothers do with clothes, a large "octopus" coal-burning furnace, and a coal bin that held a half ton of anthracite coal. The furnace consisted of the main fire pit that had grates that needed shaking periodically to drop the ashes down to a clean-out area. Coal was shoveled through a door onto the grates to be burned. Then there was a door below where you took out the ashes. Huge ducts radiated from the main part of the furnace to carry heat to the upper parts of the house.

The cellar was a place of great activity, especially in cold weather. A couple of times a week, it was necessary to take the "ash cans" to the curb for pick-up by the village Street Department. This meant hard work. The full cans were heavy. Dad and Mother had to negotiate a flight of very narrow, steep wooden steps from the cellar to a side house door and carry the ash cans to the curb. Usually there were two cans. When Hank got old enough, he helped Dad. Then I got old enough to help Hank. By the time Roger got old enough, Dad had natural gas installed. Lucky Roger!

When the gas was installed, the huge ducts were replaced with steam pipes and radiators in all of the rooms of the house. And the old coal bin was eliminated. No more did I have to help with the delivery of all that dusty, black coal. No more shoveling the coal into that huge, hungry furnace. Now we had a place for more recreational activities.

Before I go any further, let me tell you about how we entertained ourselves as kids. We did not have plastics back then. We made our own model airplanes out of balsa wood blocks, or saved enough money to buy a 10¢ kit that contained pieces of balsa wood, a block, and a flat piece, from which we carved the fuselage and wings. With some glue, decals, enamel paints (if you could afford them), and a lot of patience, you could come up with many versions of model airplanes, or boats, or cars, or lots of little pieces of balsa wood.

In the basement, Hank and I built miniature villages, airports, roadways, etc. These landscapes consisted of odds and ends of flat pieces of boards and plywood that we scrounged from the sites of new houses being built around the neighborhood. Leftover mortar was used for street paving. We molded hills and mountains, laid out streets, and formed connecting highways between various sections of the cellar.

We not only moved little lead soldier figures to portray battles, but we also rigged wires over the battlefields. Then we fastened some of our "lesser" balsa airplanes to the wires with a paper clip and sent them screaming down to drop bombs or strafe the troops. This was accomplished by first fastening a little firecracker to the airplane, timing it to drop at the "precise" moment. Or sometimes we destroyed the "enemy" plane with ground fire by flipping a small firecracker and hoping to hit one of the wire-guided airplanes. We blew up houses and had a great time. The wonder of it all, upon reflection, is that we didn't destroy our own home. We were very careful, as all little boys are, of course.

Once in a while, Mother would come to the cellar door and ask what that "popping" noise was. Or what was that odor? Of course, it was the odor of the coal burning.

When I was ten years old, my parents bought me a wood-turning lathe. By today's standards, it was very elementary. (As of this writing, I still have that lathe, and it is still in excellent working order.) This opened up a whole new world for me. It gave me an interest in woodworking, which I have enjoyed for over 60 years.

By that time, we brothers had outgrown the toy soldier stage, and Roger, being three years my junior, was not inclined that way. It was about that time that Dad bought a ping-pong table, which was a lot more of a challenge for all of us than lead soldiers being blown to bits by firecrackers.

So now we had entered the era of "Sports Arena."

The whole family learned to play ping-pong, including Mother. She was pretty good, too. I even learned to play both left-handed and right-handed. It was great family bonding time.

Then came World War II. The local pool hall on Main Street was closing its doors, so Dad, for some reason or other, decided to get one of the pool tables to place in our cellar. It was one of the old-time pool tables made of one piece of solid slate. The Turner brothers had all gone into military service, so it is still a mystery how, or by whom, that huge piece of slate ever got down those rickety, narrow, wooden stairs. But down went the whole table.

There wasn't room for both the ping-pong table and the pool table, so Dad got rid of the supports for the ping-pong table. Whenever someone wanted to play ping-pong, all you had to do was slide the folding ping-pong table on top of the pool table. Ergo! A "Sports Arena." (For your edification,

"Ergo" was a term used back in our ancient times, like you would say today "Voila!" or "So there!" or "Look what I did!" Bet you learned something today!)

After the war, when the family returned, now with the addition of my wife, Caroline, and our daughter, Sharyn, that old cellar was still a place of many memories. No matter how it changed physically, the spirit of boyhood playtime and family togetherness will remain with me forever.

OF BIRDS AND BEES

MY FIRST EXPOSURE TO the difference between men and women, and how they conduct themselves when in private surroundings, happened when I was about ten years of age. I grew up in a family consisting of my dad, mother, and two brothers. There were no sisters. But there was a lot of modesty back in the late twenties and early thirties. At least, there was supposed to be.

Girls didn't play Cops and Robbers or Cowboys and Indians, chase snakes in the grass, or other boy things. So I had no idea what girls or women wore under their dresses, or the difference in legs, etc. Mostly etc. One night, I got some indoctrination.

Each summer after school was out, my older brother Hank and I spent a week or two at a place called Occanum Falls and Inn. This was what was called a "tourist inn." It was owned by our Aunt Louise and Uncle Hugh Miller. Being located on the main road between Binghamton and New York City, it attracted a lot of tourists, going and coming.

The Occanum Inn offered picnic grounds behind the Inn, where there was a beautiful waterfall. Also, there was a very large dance hall in the main building, as well as a restaurant and a coffee shop. Only beer was for sale at the bar in the dance hall.

Overnight facilities consisted of octagon-shaped individual cabins. (Octagon-shaped cabins at Occanum Inn. Clever!) Also, there was a row of about six connected rooms just beyond the dance hall. Overall, a very nice spot for a vacation.

Hank and I would cut the grass, pump gas at 10 cents per gallon, cut the grass, clean cabins and help change linens, cut the grass, generally do anything that needed two extra hands, and did I mention: cut the grass? Incidentally, there were no power mowers back in those days. Our pay? Room and board. After all, we were family. We were told it would be fun. Funny fun, if you ask me.

Back to my story.

One night, I was asked to take some cold drinks down to one of the rooms. As I approached the room, I noticed the door was open. It was warm that night, and the screen door kept out any mosquitoes. But it did not keep in the laughter and giggling. So I walked up to the screen door and politely knocked.

As I said, it was a warm night. It must have been even warmer inside, because those six people didn't seem to be wearing very much. Maybe they were just poor. But they seemed to be dressed sort of funny.

The men were in what I recognized as undershirts and boxer shorts, like all of us men wore. The thing that surprised me was that the women were not wearing boxer shorts. Or undershirts. They seemed to have funny-shaped things strapped around their chests. Some were wearing very short shimmering "dresses" with no sleeves, just straps. And those "boxer shorts" were like nothing I had ever seen before. I'm sure all that lacy stuff had no practical purpose. It probably tickled.

Anyway, those long, smooth legs on those gals sure were pretty compared to those hairy legs of the guys. Now I knew what the older boys whistled at. I had never seen such long, shapely legs.

These people were hugging and having such a good time, rolling around on the beds. Everyone must have been smoking because the room was full of smoke. One of the women looked at me and asked if I wanted to come in.

That was mighty nice of her, but having worked all day (probably cutting grass), and it being sort of late, I unglued my eyes from those long, shapely legs and those silky-looking things that the women wore under their dresses. I thanked her, left the cold drinks, and made a dash back to the main building. Besides, those people looked like they had their hands full. (Pun intended.)

A few years later, I knew my instincts to leave were right. Another guy in the room would have made conversation sort of awkward.

Besides, I didn't smoke.

A Fish Story

THIS FISH STORY IS a true story. I know all fishermen say that. But you can believe me because I am not a fisherman. This story is not about me catching fish. It is about a method of catching fish. Usually you put bait on the hook that is at the end of a line that is fastened to the end of a pole or a more sophisticated rod and reel. Let me tell you about a method that I saw while in India, back during World War II.

We had delivered our new C-46 cargo plane to Central Command somewhere in central India. (Even if I could remember exactly where it was, I probably couldn't pronounce the name correctly.) All I remember is that we had to stay two nights and three days in this "town" that consisted of one strip of a road, along which were shops on either side. How the military found such a place to use for the delivery of replacement aircraft is beyond me. Maybe it was because it was such flat terrain, and probably because the enemy would never think of looking in a place like that.

One day, some of us decided to explore the surrounding countryside. We got a Jeep vehicle issued to us and away we went.

As we rode along, we came upon a fair-sized pond. Along one side of the pond stood a row of Indian women. At some sort of signal, all the women lowered the tops of their saris, which resembled a wrap-around sheet. (It seemed that the Indian women back in 1945 were way ahead of our

American women in the Women's Liberation Movement. Or maybe there was a shortage of bras?) Every one of those women was topless. (Not that any of us checked to be sure!)

The women all leaned over — that was a sight to behold — and lowered their sari tops to the water. Some lowered more than that! Then they all started forward, in a row.

That is when we realized the pond was not very deep. Those women walked all the way across the pond, and as they got most of the way to the other side, we saw the water start to churn.

Those women were FISHING.

When they were almost to the far side of the pond, they lifted the tops of their saris, which were acting like nets. The women proceeded to the shore and emptied their "catch" into baskets. Now that is a novel way to catch fish for that night's meal!

That night we went back to the base, rather than having a meal at the local fish house as we had planned. Spam looked pretty good after all.

A REAL SMOKER

As A PERSON GREW older and worldlier at, say, eight going on nine, it seemed only natural that certain parts of one's personality must be expanded to conform to the social customs of the day. Smoking was one of those parts of one's behavior that kept you "up to date," or "made you part of the crowd," or, as they say today, "COOL."

Back in the early thirties, tobacco had not yet been associated with cancer, so it was very much accepted.

My older brother Hank and I took one of our dad's Kaywoodie pipes. We were going to take a step toward semi-adulthood. (I think it is called Youth!) Naturally, it was Hank's idea, because I would never do such a thing. Besides, he was so much older than I. He was probably very close to 11 or 12. (I must confess, I was as eager as he was, and it was probably as much my idea as it was his. But, after all, this is my story.)

So off we went to the garage, armed with a pipe, tobacco (I don't remember if the tobacco was leftover or fresh), matches, and a lot of nerve. Big brother Hank fired up that Kaywoodie with several big puffs. Then little brother Dick (that's me) took a few puffs. It didn't taste very good, so I passed it back to Hank. After a few more puffs, poor Hank looked sort of pale. In fact, he looked rather sick. That funny look looked very unfunny. He was sick, and my stomach began to feel like Hank's face looked.

At that moment being sick was the least of our worries. At the garage door stood MOTHER!

There was poor Hank, holding one of Dad's pipes, smoke curling out of the bowl, just having taken one last puff, and probably smoke coming out of his mouth! And I had the feeling that something else was about to come out of his stomach!

Mother took Hank by the arm and marched him into the house. How dare he do such an evil thing in front of his younger brother! She would teach him a lesson he would not forget!

Little did she know that as soon as they were out of sight, I headed for the back of the garage, and was I ever sick!

To my knowledge, my noble big brother had not told on me. That taught me an even bigger lesson: the loyalty of my brother. As the old saying goes, "Put that in your pipe and smoke it."

WISDOM

It seems just a short time ago
That I would see both my parents
As my all-in-all to guide me
Through all my life and all events.

As I grew and went on to school
I found there were other folks who
Would try to be, like my parents,
My all-in-all for my life through.

My teachers, yes, even my friends
Taught me so much more, so I thought.
I realized, and I soon learned,
What they taught me was all for naught.

I drifted into those teen years,
So sure that I now knew it all.
Too bad my parents weren't like me.
When did they take that mental fall?

I now lived in a modern age,
Where values changed from "way back when,"
No longer do I need to be
Treated as a child as I had been.

My parents could not let me go.
They acted like I had no sense.
Those foolish things I seemed to do
Would be all right a few years hence.

So on I went, full of myself.
Forgetting my dear Lord above.
Not that I was ever that bad.
See, I always felt my folks' love.

They must have prayed so hard and long,
That by the time I was full-grown
I knew the things my parents taught
Are things good parents have all known.

They taught trust in the Lord above.
They taught faithfulness in the home.
They taught me: love one another,
Be honest, humble, never roam.

Suddenly I know, looking back,
What my parents had given me
Was an education far more
Valuable, because I see

How wise they were to give to me

What finally is my life's goal:
I want to share with my family,
First love, then truth, with all my soul.

Now I have grown old, wrinkled, glad
This wisdom, to our children three
From Caroline, and some from me
Is now fed back from them to me!!!

The Big Hike

WHEN I WAS ABOUT 15 years old, and a member of Troop 105 of the Boy Scouts of America, I thought that I could expand my experiences as an outdoorsman by taking a hike that was more than the 14 miles required for one of the ranks of achievement.

At that time, I lived in Johnson City, NY, a village located south of the Finger Lakes region, in the south-central part of the state.

I had a cousin who lived near Point Nell, PA, about 40 miles south of that state border. She and her husband lived on a farm in a rural area. Altogether, the cousin's farm was about 60 miles from my home.

Another boy agreed to go along with me on the hike that would satisfy that urge to "go one step further." So one fine Saturday morning we set out about 5:00 a.m., heading south. It was a beautiful summer morning. We had packed everything we thought necessary for this big hike. This included lunch and dinner for the first day, and breakfast and lunch the next. Hopefully we would be at the end of our hike in time for dinner at my cousin's house, down on the farm. Pre-packed sandwiches and fruit, and a canteen of water took care of lunch. For our dinner meal, we packed the makings of a hunter's stew: an onion, carrots, potatoes, a little Bisquick for baking a "twist" of bread, a pot to make the stew in, and our utensil kits. Breakfast would be eggs, bacon, and more Bisquick "twist."

How did we keep the food from spoiling? One of my great inventions was a portable refrigerator made of two tobacco cans: one 1-pound and one 1/2-pound can. By putting insulation material in the larger can between it and the smaller can, packing perishable foods in the small can, and freezing all of this overnight, you could keep food for at least a day, even in the sun. (On some camping trips I have kept food for two days by putting the "refrigerator" in a cool running stream in the shade.)

Our clothing needs were minimal: extra socks and rain gear. Because we were outdoorsmen, we would sleep under the stars — no tent. Besides, being "knowledgeable" outdoorsmen, we would pick a suitable, protected campsite, naturally.

Each of us had a sleeping bag: my buddy's was store-bought, mine was homemade. This hike took place around 1938 or 1939, and money was scarce. My dad got some canvas about a yard wide and probably at least ten yards long. I made my own sleeping bag, sewing it by hand, and using an old sweater zipper. I even sewed a hood over the open end and sewed some old sheer curtain net around the hood for mosquito protection. When I had the bag put together, I used blocks of paraffin wax and my mother's flat iron to waterproof the canvas. To stay warm, I simply put a blanket inside and used big safety pins to hold it in place. This may sound like crude equipment, but I used that sleeping bag until 1962, even as an adult professional staff member of the B.S.A. I used it in rain, snow, swamps, and mountains. Finally, the family decided it had to go. But it was a great sleeping bag and held many memories.

Equipped as described above, armed with mighty hatchets for preparing our campsite and hunting knives to skin any bears that we might have to kill, off we went on our big hike.

After leaving town, we crossed the Chenango Bridge and headed south. We followed the open roads for two reasons. First, there was not that much traffic on the back roads in those days. Second, we may be outdoorsmen, but we weren't stupid. Crossing all kinds of fields, streams, farms full of cows and bulls and slippery stuff, and not know where we were going anyhow? Nope! We were just going to take a big hike. Period.

We had covered about seven or eight miles when near disaster struck. My pack frame failed! The pad that kept the wooden main part of the frame off my back (and rested at belt level on my hips) came loose and made it pretty uncomfortable to balance the homemade canvas pack, hand-sewn, impregnated with wax, etc.—you know all about that by now, don't you? It seemed that my new and improved, two-touch, lightweight, easy-to-make pack frame needed a few refinements. Being the inventor that I was, and determined to complete my big hike, somehow I got the thing back together with lashings, and on we went. Too bad we didn't have duct tape back in those days.

Down the road we walked. Occasionally, an automobile would drive by. A couple even stopped to ask if we needed a ride. Having driven with my family to my cousin's farm a couple of times, I was able to remember some of the landmarks. My goal was to get to one such historical landmark: a tremendous stone railroad bridge. It may still be standing. It must have been hundreds of feet high and from one mountain to another.

It reminded me of those ancient viaducts built by the Romans, standing about four stone arches high. That was where we would spend the night, camped on the bank of a stream, in an open field. We started a fire and prepared our evening meal. Having walked for about ten hours, including rest and a lunch break, it was nice just to relax, our bellies full of really good food. It was a beautiful evening, a night under the stars, and no threat of rain. Life was so simple and peaceful. I'm tempted to say, "the good old days." So we settled into our sleeping bags and slept till dawn. (No bears.)

After our great breakfast, and after cleaning up our campsite, making sure the fire was completely out, we set off on the rest of our big hike.

It was shortly after lunchtime that we arrived at the farm. Of course, they knew we were coming. We spent a couple of days working with Ken, my cousin's husband. We milked the cows, helped bring in the hay, chopped firewood for the kitchen range, slopped the hogs, helped clean the barn, and wandered all over the place. It was wonderful. Lots of work, but with a sense of freedom and belonging.

I even learned how to put the "twist" in the axe as it hit a large piece of wood, thereby splitting a piece at least 14 to 16 inches in diameter, and up to 18 inches long. We went to bed each night tired but eager to get back to work again in the morning.

On the weekend, my parents drove down to the farm to pick us up and take us back home. It had been a great experience, and I suppose I had satisfied that urge to "go one step farther." To take a long hike.

But I think I learned a lot more. Take time to look around and see what God has created for us in nature and in the talents of mankind. Relax once in a while and "do the chores of the farm." Learn something new — even if you don't think you will ever use the knowledge. Stretch your eyes — maybe you will see a vision. Stretch your mind — maybe you will hear what God has to say.

You may not take a big hike by walking, but you may find other ways to take your own BIG HIKE.

Caroline's Humor

WHILE CAROLINE WAS IN the rehabilitation unit at the Sardis Nursing Facility in Charlotte, NC, in November 2000, we were waiting for lunch to be brought to her. We were in the dining room. At one of the adjacent tables, we overheard one of the ladies ask her visitor if she would like to have a chair to sit in while she visited with her.

Caroline leaned over to me and said, "No. She wants to sit on the floor."

Caroline was employed by the Regional office of the American Red Cross in Charlotte, in the Public Relations Department. She worked in an all-woman office as the Administrative Assistant to the Director.

She loved working with the "girls", and evidently they loved Caroline. She was older than all the others, and I suppose they respected her for the way she sort of "kept them in line" as to manners, protocol, and language. Whenever one of her fellow (or should I say female) workers used some foul word or told a sleazy story, they knew Caroline would get after them.

After just so much of this, Caroline went out and bought a bar of old-fashioned Octagon soap, which she kept in one of her desk drawers. It was amazing how much the girls cleaned up their language, because whenever one of them said a bad word, Caroline would whip out her bar of soap and plop it down on her desk!

Evidently all of those girls had heard, as children, about getting their mouths washed out with soap if they used bad words.

Pretty soon the girls could be heard saying, "Better not use that word, or tell that story, Caroline will wash your mouth out with her bar of Octagon soap!"

It worked!

Since I Became a Pile of Scrap Metal

MARCH 24, 2002

Many years ago, when just a kid,
The dentist opened my mouth and said:
"I'm gonna drill a hole in that tooth
And put some metal inside your head."

Well, since that day so long, long ago,
More holes have been drilled into my teeth.
More metal has gone into the top
And even some in the row beneath.

The metal they use is some alloy.
I'm not sure what kind: iron? tin?
All I know is, the dentist can sure
Drill holes and then pack the metal in.

As if that isn't enough metal
To make one's mouth clatter and quiver,
In latter years, trying to save teeth,

They capped some with pure gold and silver.

Then came the time in my later life
When I had to get a brand new hip.
The ball part had deteriorated.
It got no blood, not even a drip.

So a new artificial ball and joint.
Made of plastic, and of course, metal,
Looking like an old-time railroad spike,
Would await me in the hospital.

They put me to sleep one early morn,
Flesh and bone, with metal in my teeth.
When I came to, they said, "Don't you move.
Surgery took an hour, two or threeth."

"You got metal in that brand new hip,
So don't you dare move around so hard.
You got enough metal in you now,
You qualify to be a junk yard!"

Now when I fly, the alarms go off!
My teeth and hip the alarms unsettle!!!
That is how my life has now become,
Since I became a pile of scrap metal!!!

FLYING BLIND

As I approached Wilmington, NC, that early morning of October 28, 1944 — just 20 days after my wedding on the 8th of that month — I was flying at about 500 feet of altitude. As I recognized the landmarks below, I was able to fly directly over 1705 Ann Street. Sure enough, I saw my bride, now Mrs. Caroline Davis Turner, walk out of her parents' home, on her way to the airfield to get me. I wiggled my wings frantically, but she did not look up. After all, this was wartime, and there were lots of military planes in the air all the time. I had been stationed at the airfield when I met the love of my life on August 26 of that same year. One more plane was — well, just one more plane.

My new assignment was at Camp Stewart, GA, outside of Savannah. I was flying tow-targets for the anti-aircraft artillery to practice shooting at. That was the first time I ever saw "flack" AHEAD of my plane. They sure needed more practice that day! The airbase commander allowed me to have one of the BT-13 tracking planes to fly to Wilmington to see my bride. I'm not sure how he justified the use of the plane. Perhaps it was for a "secret counter-intelligence, diplomatic, surreptitious, pre-peace planning meeting for the post-war civilian era." As long as he said to go, I felt it my duty to obey his orders.

It was wonderful to see my Caroline again. It had been two weeks since I last saw her, so we made every moment count!

On Sunday, it was time to part again. We made plans for Caroline to come stay with me at the Officers' Guest House the next week. I had purchased a 1940 two-door Pontiac the previous week from another pilot who had received orders to ship out. We would then go back to Wilmington in the near future and tow her father's trailer home to my new assignment. Living conditions were not very acceptable around the base, and Caroline certainly was not going to be able to stay in the Officers' barracks!

At the airfield, Old Hot Pilot climbed into his airplane, waved to his bride, and taxied out to the runway. With full throttle, and with a last-second leap into the air, I flew into the wild blue yonder. Giving a last wiggle of my wings, I headed back to my duty to win the war, filled with memories of a beautiful weekend with the love of my life.

I headed south-by-southwest to Hunter Field at Camp Stewart, via Charleston, SC. All was well as I approached Charleston until a couple of black specks appeared on the front of the canopy. Then the spots turned into a blur. It looked like oil. If it was oil, it was time to get on the ground fast. Finding the radio frequency for Charleston, I contacted the airfield control tower. After I explained my problem, I requested clearance for an emergency landing. It was granted, so down I went.

By that time, I could not see out the front of my plane. Using partial instruments and partial side visibility, I put the Vultee Vibrator (so-called by student pilots because it really seemed to shake all the time we were in the air, like a wet dog shakes off water) into a "crab." In this attitude, the airplane is aimed in one direction and flying in another. The trick is to be sure to "kick out of the crab" before the wheels touch the runway.

Everything has to be coordinated so the plane is going straight down the runway! Otherwise you shear off the landing gear. That is frowned upon. Especially if the pilot is an Old Hot Pilot Second Lieutenant! Yes, I took the plane out of the "crab" and landed safely. We found out later that the mechanic back at the airfield in Wilmington had not secured the oil-filler cap.

It is well that I managed to get the plane on the ground quickly because engines seem to require oil. It is difficult to pull over to get more oil when up in the air. There don't seem to be any service stations up there.

Time to get back into the air again. After thanks for the help, once again, I was off into the wild blue yonder. This time I was heading more to the West, more into the sun. It was getting towards evening, and the sun was lower on the horizon. That is when everything seemed very hazy. In fact, I could not make out any details ahead of me. Then it struck me! Although the canopy had been cleaned off, apparently they had left a film of oil on it. It is difficult to get oil off plexiglas, so I do not fault the ground crew.

But that did not help my situation. Again, no service stations up there, and it is quite difficult to stop and clean off the windshield. Especially at a couple of thousand feet in the air!

For the second time that day, I was flying blind. However, my instrument flight training must have registered. Using my Flight Plan and my radio, I was able to zero in on my destination, Hunter Field. As I got close enough, the sun was setting, and I had lowered my altitude enough that the sun no longer put a glare on the canopy, enabling me to land safely!

Some may say it was my good training that got me back safely. I now prefer to tell you that God and His angels had to be with me when I was flying blind. I have learned that the more I trust Him and call on Him, the more He continues to save me, as I am still so often "flying blind."

Boy Scouting

AT THE AGE OF 12, many boys joined the Boy Scouts of America. Specifically, they joined a group called a troop.

When I became 12 years of age, my parents allowed, even encouraged, me to join the troop where my big brother Hank was already a member. The troop was sponsored by the Primitive Methodist Church in Johnson City, NY. I do not remember the name of the Scoutmaster, the adult leader of this Troop 3. Nor do I remember how many boys belonged to this troop. What I show below comes from records that I have saved all of these years, never dreaming that I would someday incorporate them in a book for my family.

I joined the troop on or about March 23, 1936, nine days after my 12th birthday. I finished the requirements for the rank of Tenderfoot on April 4 of that year and started working on the requirements for the next rank, Second Class.

At some point, I left scouting. Why, I do not remember. But apparently, in late 1937 or January of 1938, I joined Troop 105, sponsored by the Baptist Church on Main Street in Johnson City. It was over two miles from my home, but I walked to meetings every week, and sometimes in between for special events. Rain, snow, or whatever the weather was, I seldom missed a meeting or event of Troop 105. Perhaps it was the program. Or perhaps the relationships with other Scouts. But I look back now and realize it was more than likely my Scoutmaster, who allowed me and other troop members to do the best we could.

Mr. Cliff Springer did not look like a Scoutmaster. He was almost bald, overweight — especially at the mid-drift -- and did not own a uniform. But then, neither did we Scouts have official uniforms. Our uniforms consisted of WWI leggings, canteens, cartridge belts, breeches, and a smattering of B.S.A. shirts.

One piece of uniform was official: our neckerchief, indicating our troop color and design. Shoes were whatever our parents could afford, to be used for school, church, or hiking. Cliff, as we called our Scoutmaster, had a rag-tag troop of boys, but we were always in the top honors at the competitive events that were held all over our county.

We could tie knots faster, treat the "wounded" better in First Aid, signal with flags or Morse code faster and with fewer mistakes, lash poles into bridges stronger, etc., than all the competition. Why? We were from Troop 105!

As a result of all of this training and going camping a couple of times a month in all kinds of weather, I earned my Second Class rank on March 1, 1938. My next goal was the First Class rank, which I achieved on May 3, 1938. From this time on, I would work on my leadership skills, service, and the required merit badges for the ranks of Star, Life, and finally that coveted rank of Eagle Scout.

I received the rank of Star in August of 1938 after completing the requirements in the Wood Work, Wood Carving, Carpentry, Public Health, and Personal Health merit badges, and three months service. Some of these were required badges.

I was awarded the rank of Life Scout on December 5, 1938. This meant that I had to earn at least five more merit badges — First Aid, Athletics, Handicraft, Signaling, and the Life Saving — plus three more months of leadership and service. But there was still that rank of Eagle that only about

5% of scouts attain. The challenge was there. I really wanted to become an Eagle.

I earned the next seven required merit badges: Swimming, Cooking, Camping, Civics, Bird Study, Path Finding, and Safety. Add to this, merit badges in Pioneering, Firemanship, Electricity, and Art, and six more months to prove my leadership qualities and service to my family, fellow Scouts, and my community. On June 6, 1939, I was presented with my Eagle Badge and Certificate. The local newspaper even gave me a write-up for my efforts.

I went on to earn these other merit badges as follows:

Public Speaking

Salesmanship

Business

Airplane Structure

Music

Automobiling

Painting

Masonry

Book Binding

Reading

Machinery

Architecture

Aviation

Sculpture

Weather

Hiking

Surveying

Plumbing

Farm Layout

Aeronautics

First Aid to Animals

Basketry

Photography

Leather craft

Scholarship

Farm Home

Reptile Study

Metal Work

Animal Industry

Gardening

The required number of merit badges needed for Eagle was 21. For each five additional merit badges earned, you received a Bronze Palm Leaf, a Gold Palm Leaf, and then a Silver Palm Leaf. The extra 30 merit badges that I received entitled me to wear a double set of Bronze, Gold, and Silver Palm Leaves on the ribbon of my Eagle Badge.

After WWII, my wife Caroline and our children lived in Wilmington, N.C., where we were members of Trinity Methodist Church, which sponsored a Boy Scout Troop. I became active as an adult leader and held various positions in the local council of the B.S.A.

I was the Training Chairman of the Cape Fear Council, served as a Commissioner, and later became an Explorer Scout Leader. I even held a leadership position in a Sea Scout Ship. (Kids, that little statuette was presented to me as "Outstanding Scouter Award.")

Then it was my privilege to serve as the Cub master of our church-sponsored Cub Pack. As an adult volunteer, I was awarded the Scouter's Award and the Scouter's Key.

In 1959, I was asked to consider becoming a Professional Scouter, working for the National program of the Boy Scouts of America.

After completing my training at the Schiff Scout Reservation for full-time Scout employees, I was accepted as a District Scout Executive (DSE) in the Blue Ridge Council, Greenville, SC. My family and I moved to Anderson, SC.

From there we moved to Lakeland, FL, for my next assignment. We served there for five years, a record. The Mayor even gave Caroline and me the Keys to the City of Lakeland when we left. It was a great assignment in the Gulf Ridge Council.

The next move took our family to the Georgia-Carolina Council, headquartered in Augusta, GA. We lived in Aiken, SC, where we set another tenure record of 5 years. It was during this assignment that I took a group of older Scouts to the Philmont Scout Reservation in NM. I also developed a new Wilderness Camp for the Council on Clark Hill Reservoir, which was another memorable assignment.

My last position with the B.S.A. was in Charlotte, NC, as the DSE of a multi-man District.

During these years, I completed the National Camp School, completed and earned my Beads for Wood-badge, my Five-Year Training Award, the Fifty Miler, and Historic Trails Awards. I organized over 30 local Camporees and numerous Scout and Adult Scouter indoor and outdoor training courses.

Having completed the Professional Scouter Basic and the Intermediate Programs, it was my privilege to receive my Fellowship Training Award after a ten-year program of study and application of financial, leadership, and other courses that apply to working with and for volunteers, in service-related programs.

Also, I was awarded all three degrees from the Order of the Arrow: Ordeal, Brotherhood, and the coveted Vigil Honor. My Indian name is Weuksowagen (one who has knowledge).

I left the Boy Scouts of America in 1974, both as a Professional and a Volunteer, and took a position with the American Red Cross, from which I retired in 1989.

Fish Story #2

While I was in India during World War II, another pilot and I had the opportunity to get a Jeep and go into the nearby town of Dibrugarh, several miles from our airbase at Mohanbari. We were in the Assam Valley, among the great tea plantations. This is in what was northeast India, near the foothills of the Himalayan Mountains.

The road was gravel, maintained by the military. Alongside was a ditch about six to eight feet deep, in which there was drain and run-off water. The muddy water was perhaps only a foot deep. The ditch was necessary during the monsoon season to carry off the torrential rains. At this time, it was not the monsoon season.

As we drove along, we came upon some kind of operation on the side of the road. Curious, we stopped to see what was going on with that group of Indians. There was some sort of wooden trestle built over the ditch, to which was fastened a rope. A few feet beyond the trestle, there was a platform over the ditch, where a couple of men were emptying a good-sized bucket of mud and water over a screen. After they emptied the bucket, which was tied to the rope that was fastened to the trestle, one of the men tossed it over the side, where it fell down to the water level. Another couple of men caught the bucket and scooped it full of mud and water. In the meantime, the men on the platform were going through the contents on the screen, removing something and putting whatever it was into another bucket. Then the men on the trestle hauled the freshly loaded bucket up from below and dumped more residue on the screen.

It looked very efficient and coordinated. One of the engineering wonders of the world.

These men were FISHING!

We discovered, upon asking, these men were indeed catching tiny fish from that run-off ditch, to be divided among those who were using their ingenuity to provide food for their families. This, too, is a true fish story.

THE HUNTER

COME WITH ME, WHEN I was a young lad of about 14, back to the mid-thirties, before the outbreak of World War II. The Great Depression was not yet over, but people were beginning to have some hope that the real tough times were easing somewhat. Men were getting jobs building some of the great infrastructure of this nation, as part of the government-sponsored programs, the results of which we all enjoy today. There were not as many dollars available, but each one had far greater value than they have today.

When I was 12 years old, I joined the Boy Scouts of America, Troop No. 105. My parents, two brothers, and I (one older and one younger) lived in the village of Johnson City, NY. This is still a village located in the south-central part of the state, at the junction of the Chenango and Susquehanna Rivers, near the foothills of the Catskill Mountains, south of the Finger Lakes.

The geography lesson is almost over, unless you quit reading all of this story. The reason for all of this is so you can get oriented to the environment in which I was raised.

We did not have such things as plastic (molded into things or in card form), so many of the extras in life had to be substituted, or handmade by the ones who couldn't do without. There just wasn't the money to use on things other than food, clothing, shelter, and the necessities of life. If you wanted something bad enough, you had to earn extra money, get a rich uncle to subsidize you, or make it yourself. Stealing was frowned on. And illegal.

I wanted a bow and some arrows.

One of the merit badges in Scouting was Archery. A bow and arrow could be fun, a skill to be developed, and if proficient, a scout could have another award towards that coveted rank of Eagle Scout. Besides, the Indians used the bow and arrow to provide meat for the family table. The woods in the area abounded with rabbits, squirrels, pheasants, and even deer. What an accomplishment if I could provide meat for the Turner table! I had hunted for rabbits and squirrels, and even shot a few with Dad's 410 shotgun. But think of the satisfaction if I brought home a DEER, shot with a bow and arrow!

Ah, youth.

But we did not have the money for store-bought archery equipment. What to do?

At age 12, I was gainfully employed by the grocery store, down the block from where we lived. I delivered the weekly Sales Specials flyers to all of the houses in what seemed to be at least 20 square miles. Actually, it was probably only about 25 or 30 square blocks. The size seemed to change according to the weather. In the summer and spring, it seemed to be only 50 to 60 blocks. In the cooler days and in the winter, it had to be at least 20 square miles.

The pay wasn't bad. I received 50 cents weekly. Nice part was that it was all tax-free. Remember, this was just after the Depression. My dad was a ladies' shoe designer and pattern maker at Endicott-Johnson Shoe Co., a skilled worker, highly paid at $22 a week. That was good pay in those days!

Through the Boy Scout catalogue, I purchased a piece of lemonwood, from which I would fashion my own bow. It cost a couple of dollars. But I had MONEY. Then I had to buy the linen string from which I had to weave the bowstring. (It would be hard to shoot a deer without the bowstring.) Of course, a bowstring had to be waxed during and after its manufacture. Now I had a little less MONEY.

That six-foot-long piece of lemonwood could not be bent in its rough form, so I had to buy a spokeshave. A spokeshave is like a wood plane, except the "plate" where the blade comes through, is only a couple of inches long. A wood plane has a "plate" from several inches to upwards of a couple of feet. The purpose of the spokeshave is to be able to cut the excess wood away to make an irregular or curved shape in the wood.

Enough of the Industrial Arts class. All I knew was that I sure ran out of MONEY fast. And I still didn't have the shafts, fletching, or points for the arrows. Now you may know why earlier I told you about having to improvise to get the things you "had to have."

After delivering a trillion or more flyers for the grocery man, over many square miles, I got enough money to buy the spokeshave, a couple of arrow shafts, and some arrow points, both target and hunting points. After all, wasn't I going to provide meat for the table? As far as needing fletching for the arrows, that was simple: turkey feathers.

Finally, I had all of the needed tools and materials to become a Hunter. With my spokeshave, I fashioned my bow. It is necessary to keep testing the strength, or "pull" of a bow. A homemade one can be made to fit the ability of the archer. A store-bought bow is whatever "pull" the manufacturer creates. The purchaser tries to get a bow to fit his or her needs, or as closely as possible. My bow was finally tested at 60 pounds. Not bad for a skinny 110-pounder. But I had made it just for me.

After I finished my bow and had made some arrows (a few had the razor-sharp flat blades to hunt that deer, for meat for the table), I was ready to try my abilities as an archer. This meant target practice.

There was just enough distance from the front of our property to the back of our yard for me to get close to those enviable 30 paces, for which Robin Hood became famous. At the back of the yard, my mother had her beautiful rose bushes. That was an incentive to be sure to hit the canvas target that I erected. More MONEY.

Back and forth I went: shoot those few arrows, retrieve those few arrows. Shoot again. Retrieve again. Too bad I ran out of MONEY to buy the material to make more arrows.

But practice never hurt anyone who wants to achieve a certain goal. Believe it or not, I got my skill level up to where I not only earned my Archery merit badge, but I was able to split a cigarette at that distance. No, I was not on an anti-smoking campaign. Nor did I smoke. I was too young. (My parents asked that we brothers not smoke till we were out of high school.)

Time to put that meat on the table.

A few trips into the woods with my trusty bow and arrows convinced me that the animals must have been forewarned of my coming. They must have been frightened to death, because they seemed to all stay way beyond the range of my weapon. Even so, I was able to get a few shots off at what I was sure had to be a very large (meaty) deer or bear. Maybe it was a mountain lion, fox or cougar. Just think of how my hunting trips may have protected lots of lives of animals and people. I am sure they were not those cows that sometimes roamed out of the pastures. Unfortunately, I never did find those arrows. Not only did I lose arrows, but there goes more MONEY.

Well, hunting with a bow and arrows got old after a while.

Let me jump into another phase in the life of this hunter.

My mother had a sister who lived in Pennsylvania, in a community called Springfield, near Moscow. Actually, it wasn't a community, or not one that I ever saw. We are back into that geography lesson again. Perhaps you get the idea that she lived in the country. Her name was Eva, married to Uncle Win Scott, who provided meat for the family table by hunting for squirrels, rabbits, woodchucks, and other small animals.

When we visited Aunt Eva, Uncle Win, and lots of cousins, we were treated to some real woodsy food. What a chance for Hunter (that's me) to go off with his uncle, into the woodlands of upper Pennsylvania, and perhaps provide meat for the family table, with his trusty and mighty 60-pound bow and his lethal arrows. Naturally, the next time we visited the Scott residence, I took my Hunter equipment.

As I recall, Uncle Win wasn't going hunting during this visit. I was not able to go hunting by myself, being unfamiliar with that area. So there would not be meat on the family table on this visit.

But hear what happened!

The Scott family, being very self-sufficient, raised chickens and hogs. No, Hunter was not about to shoot a hog! But a chicken? Yeah!!!

It was decided to have chicken for supper. The normal way to kill a chicken is to wring its neck. But what if you have Hunter there, with his mighty bow, who could split a cigarette at 30 paces? Yes, let Hunter kill the chicken.

A proper chicken was selected from all those running all over the backyard. Hunter got his bow. An arrow was selected, one that would fly straight and true, with a sharp hunting point at its tip. Taking a hunter's stance, Hunter stood straight and lifted his bow. Then he nocked his arrow. (That is Archer talk for the uninitiated. It is the act of putting the notched end of the arrow to the bowstring.)

Hunter put his fingers to the bowstring, held the arrow, and aimed at that chicken, probably already knowing how that meat would taste. At last, he and his homemade archery equipment were going to be put to the real test. Hunter knew many people were watching and were depending on his prowess as an archer to provide meat for the family table that night.

Fearless and confident was Hunter. The bowstring was pulled. The mighty bow was bent to its mighty "mightiness," and the formidable arrow was aimed at the heart of that chicken. Actually, Hunter didn't have a clue where the heart of the chicken was, and still doesn't (sounds good, tho'), but that arrow was released. Through the air it sped, true to its mark. That poor chicken didn't know what hit it. A direct hit!!!

We all enjoyed a chicken dinner that night.

Hunter had at last put meat on the family table with his bow and arrow.

Shop Talk

ABOUT SCROLL SAWS AND LIFE

HAVE YOU EVER TRIED to cut a piece of wood on a scroll saw? A scroll saw is the kind of saw with which you can make curved cuts on pieces of wood, or some other materials. The blade is usually very thin or narrow. It is secured by an upper and lower clamp arrangement, with the blade passing through a slot in a table, on which you guide the piece of work.

If you push the piece of work too hard, you jam the work, break the blade, go off the line that you wanted to follow, or lose your cool. (Translated: temper.) So it is in life. Slow down and be deliberate, know where you are headed, and "stay on the line."

The easiest way to do that is to pray before you ever start a project. Ask the Lord to guide and direct you, and when you have finished, give credit and thanks to the Lord.

A NAIL ON THE HEAD

How many times have you had to put a nail in a very specific place, lined it up, and raised your hammer, knowing you had just one chance to "do it right?" Then the hammer slid off the nail head and left that little dimple in the wood.

How many times have you been putting nails in some project, one after another? And then the next time you try to replace a nail that must have been defective, the one that bent, you find that the manufacturer must have gotten a supply of cheap material. The next couple of nails also bent!

Lots of times in life, we come across situations where "nails seem to be bent," where our plans don't seem to go where we want them to go.

I found that when I had bent a nail, literally, in my woodworking, I needed to stop and ask for the guidance of the Lord. Honestly, every time this happened, I was able to hit the nail squarely on its head and drive it straight in place. In fact, many times I have used the talents of the Lord when I knew I was in a tight spot. Pre-planning at its best!

Next time you are in a tight spot, or have "bent a nail" along life's way, take time to ask the Lord to help you "drive the nail straight." In fact, it is a good practice to always ask the Lord to guide you in anything you do.

THE LOCKED DOOR

WHEN I SEE A commercial airplane being loaded with passengers, or see an airliner flying overhead, I have flashbacks of some of the missions that we had to fly during World War II. It is in those flashbacks that I remember most of our missions were flown with a pilot, a co-pilot, and a radio operator. But sometimes we, too, carried a planeload of human beings.

I was stationed in the China-Burma-India Theater of the war. We flew from a base named Mohanbari in the Assam Valley, over the Himalayan Mountains of India, Burma, and China, and to bases in these countries. Hence, the name of that theater of war, also called the CBI. Also, we had affectionate names for that big pile of rocks: the "Hump," the "Rock Pile," the "Aluminum-Clad Trail," the "Widow-Maker," and a few that I will not share with you on this page.

The missions were combat-rated because there were still enemy aircraft operating from outlying bases in Burma and China. They could harass us as we delivered all the materials of war needed by our Army, Air Force, and even the Navy. We were the original airlift, the forerunner of the way war is fought today.

It was necessary to get the ground troops as close as possible to the fighting, so they could eliminate those threats to the Allied operation. We only carried Chinese soldiers.

Each time we flew troops, for some reason, they were put aboard prior to those of us who were to fly the airplane. This was a problem for me, because those poor soldiers had no seats. They just seemed to squat on the floor of the plane, sort of scattered about. When we boarded, it was necessary to thread our way around, over, through, and past all of those Chinese troops who were staring intently at us.

I often wondered whether it was awe, fear, distrust, or amazement in their eyes. They probably wondered about this 21-year-old skinny white guy with no beard who was going to take them for a ride way up in the air. And they didn't even have parachutes. But they all had rifles!!! And bayonets!!! That was enough to make sure we got to the cockpit in a hurry. But we tried to be reassuring: we carried no parachutes with us as we boarded the plane. And, of course, we locked the cockpit door after we boarded. It was just a small latch, but we LOCKED THE DOOR.

It made us feel better!

It is true about the beard. I tried my best to grow a mustache when I was overseas, but there just wasn't enough fuzz to help me look like a carefree, seasoned, war-weary combat hot pilot. By the time I got into civilian life, and the whiskers grew enough to be slightly seen, my wife Caroline said if I grew a beard or mustache, I could sleep on the couch.

Harrumph! I showed her! I took her right to bed!!! (After I shaved.)

Back to India.....

My concern was for those poor soldiers in case we had engine failure or some other reason to have to abandon our plane. They would have no chance of survival. But then, neither would we, if we had to put on our parachutes and leave the cockpit, and head for the cargo door at the rear of the plane. Can you imagine what those eyes would look like if we attempted to walk past them and reach for the door? And those bayonets looked very sharp!

We solved that problem by having our chutes put in the cockpit before they loaded the troops. Not that we had much chance of squeezing out through the lower cargo hatch beneath the cockpit. I sure am glad we were never put to the test. But mostly, I am glad for the sake of those poor Chinese soldiers. They would have enough problems after they got off at our destination.

So the memories remain. We wear no parachutes when we fly on our modern commercial airliners.

But neither do our pilots. The memories provoke the thoughts I recall of the responsibility that goes with our pilots. These people are truly the most unsung, taken-for-granted, under-appreciated servants to the traveling public. We are at the mercy of their abilities, but they are the ones who carry the responsibility for not only their airplane and themselves, but for each of us who sits in a seat on their airplane.

When you pray for safety next time you fly, don't forget to include the flight crew, too.

SEPARATED TOGETHERNESS

MAY 19, 2002

We were newly weds, about eight weeks when
Caroline did such a beautiful thing:
One of those little things only she would
Do. So about her praises I must sing.

They gave me a ten-day delay en-route,
To get married and have a honeymoon,
Before reporting to my next air base.
I hoped not to go overseas too soon.

I was an Army Air Corps pilot who
Fell in love with this pretty Southern Belle.
I knew on the night we had that blind date,
I would marry Caroline. I could tell.

She was all I could ever want and love,
Five-feet three, in her pretty black lace dress,
One hundred three pounds of my heart's desire.
Instant love of this brunette, I confess.

After a few weeks, with no place to rent,
Her Dad said we should tow down to that base
A trailer home he kept down on the beach.
Little rent, privacy, just the right place.

With our "new" used Pontiac car I bought,
We two lovebirds towed our very first home
To that Air Base and set up our love nest.
Now to explain the title of this poem.

We settled into her dad's trailer home,
Thanksgiving Day was that week, if you please.
Caroline prepared a chicken, gravy,
Sweet potatoes, and mixed carrots and peas.

She had rolls, butter, mustard pickles, too.
Coffee and pie waited. Oh, what a sight!
But Caroline already knew, carrots
I would eat, but were not my favorite.

My sweet Caroline, just before we ate,
Unbeknown, unsuspecting, if you please;
She separated the carrots for her,
And she served, just for me, all of those peas!

So Caroline taught me this sweet lesson:
God gave me a loving wife He did bless.
By separating those carrots and peas,
Love proved: Separated Togetherness.

MID-ATLANTIC STAG MOVIE

A FTER THE WORLD WAR II hostilities stopped, those of us who were still overseas were most anxious to get back to our loved ones. My beautiful bride, Caroline, and our four-month-old first child, Sharyn Elizabeth, were waiting for me in Caroline's hometown of Wilmington, NC.

Finally, my name appeared on the list to return. A group of us was put aboard an airplane at our home base of Mohanbari, India, in the Assam valley, located west of the foothills of the Himalaya Mountains. This had been the airfield from which I had made 72 1/2 combat missions into Burma and China. It was time to go home.

The airplane took us to Karachi, India, to wait for a ship to carry us to New York City, where the military would transfer us to a staging base, and then relieve us from active duty. Officers did not get discharged; just relieved of active duty. (I often wondered what would happen if they tried to find us and put us back on active duty. I think my response would be, "I forgot how to fly, Sir." Or "What is an airplane, Sir?")

Karachi is on the West Coast of India. Weeks went by. The only nice part that I remember was the real meat that was served at the Officers' Club. Real steak.

After we had been there several weeks, some of us went on a fishing trip in the Indian Ocean. There were about six or eight of us, and a crew of four Indians. We went on a dhow, or single-mast fishing boat. After we had all taken a swim, diving into the clear, cool water, some of the guys put lines out to try to catch fish for lunch. The Indians had a charcoal brazier burning, just in case. No one caught a fish for our lunch. The only catch was a baby shark about 18 inches long. I took a picture to prove this story. After throwing the shark back, I got to wondering: what if Mama shark had come looking for Baby shark while we were swimming! At least we had hot tea. Speak of gourmet cuisine!

For six weeks, we waited in Karachi. Come to find out, we could not leave because of the striking dock workers in New York City! That really made us mad. We wished we had those guys over with us. I believe in people's rights, but we had been overseas protecting those rights. The rights did not include greed at a time like that.

In the meantime, we waited. There was a brick wall outside the BOQ where we stayed. At night, the top of that wall was lined with Indian kids, who serenaded us with contemporary American songs — in English! They didn't know the meaning of the words, and some of that singing was really bad, but they had enthusiasm! No one knows how they learned those songs, but it provided some humor.

When it finally came time to leave the exotic world of the China-Burma-India Theater of war, many images remained in my memory, other than the separation from family and home. The poverty, most of all. The street-side snake charmers, the untouchables, the deformed having to beg, women washing clothes in streams, on the rocks (not a drink!), the cremations in public places.

But other sights like the beauty of the Himalayas, our tent boy (about 45 to 50 years old) who served us so faithfully every day for nine months, in spite of how we "ugly Americans" acted (when we left, we four pitched in and made him almost wealthy by local standards); the huge stretches of tea plantations, and the culture of the Indian people — strange to us, but meaningful to them. Yes, memories, but I was willing to put it all in the past. I was really ready to go home, to my way of life, with my own family.

When we got to the docks, it took hours of waiting in lines in the tropical sun to get to the ship. The name on its bow was the *M.S. Torrens*. It was of Norwegian registry, being a motor ship tanker, converted to a troop carrier. I didn't care if it was from Timbuktu, as long as it would float and know the quickest route home. The lines of men had to be certified, guided to the inevitable paperwork sections, and then directed to the gangplank for boarding. That gangplank was about three feet wide, had rope rails, and went up to the ship at an angle that must have been at least thirty degrees. Because the ship was yet to be fully loaded, it sat high in the water. Hence the steep angle.

At that moment, I was almost tempted to throw my gear over the side of the dock. I had a B-4 bag (like a heavy folding canvas garment bag) carrying my extra uniforms, a duffel bag (carrying more clothing), a leather satchel carrying the sandstone and marble Taj Mahal, and other souvenirs, and another leather case with all my Orders and Papers.

Perhaps I could maneuver up the gangplank with most of that stuff, but what about the extra duffel bag? To this day, I do not know how I got up that impossibly narrow, swinging, steep entry to that ship, except that at one time I happened to look down. That sight was enough incentive to carry me the rest of the way. I was a 128-pound nervous wreck when I got on the deck of that ship.

We were assigned to one of the holds where canvas bunks, five high, became our home for the next 32 days.

The trip through the Indian Ocean, Red Sea, Suez Canal, and across the Mediterranean Sea was very interesting, and passing through the Strait of Gibraltar was simply a passageway to the great Atlantic Ocean, and that was a clear shot to the good old U.S.A.

The Atlantic Ocean is much rougher sailing than the other bodies of water, which I mentioned before. We did fairly well about a third of the way across. Then we ran into a tremendous storm, the story of which must be told elsewhere. What a relief to get into calmer waters and weather!

By now, you must be wondering about that stag movie mentioned in the title of this story. Here it comes.

One night, I climbed the ladder and went on deck to get some fresh air. As I cleared the hatch, I looked out to sea, and then I looked forward toward the bridge of the ship. I could not believe my eyes! I was having illusions! Battle, fatigue --- except there was no battle!

I saw naked women dancing in mid-air!!!

Perhaps being separated from the female gender for so long caused me to get overly anxious. But then I realized those naked women were being projected on the back of the tall, white bridge of the ship. I was an old man of 21, married, a father, and had been exposed to lots of earthy stories, but never had I seen a stag movie until that night in the middle of the Atlantic Ocean. I had come right from high school into the Air Corps. There wasn't much opportunity for such things, unless you went looking for them. After all, it had been wartime.

After studying the figures on the "screen," I was sure they were indeed female. And they did not have on any clothes. Funny how I was concerned that they might catch a cold. Some of them did have goose bumps.

Apparently, some of the higher command thought we might need a lesson in what we might face when we got home to our loved ones. Or perhaps they thought some of us might go to medical school, and this would give us a head start in anatomy. Maybe they thought we had forgotten what a woman looked like. Well, it didn't faze me one bit. I had a good memory. Besides, I was on my way home, and was a very patient person.

However, I did go to one of the lifeboats, got out one of the oars, leaned over the side of the ship, and started to paddle as fast as I could.

My sweet wife Caroline was back home, and I was on my way to see her and our new daughter.

Time to Close or Open my Eyes

One summer back in the 1970s, our good friends, Bo and Lib Dyches, asked Caroline and me to share their condo at the Magic Tree Resort in Kissimmee, Florida. It is located just outside the gates of Walt Disney World.

The four of us had done this before, so we were familiar with many of the attractions. We still liked to go to our favorite rides, shows, and events. However, on this day, Bo decided he wanted to stay at the condo, swim in the pool, soak up some Florida sunshine, and just be lazy. Fine. But Lib, Caroline, and I wanted to take in one last day at the theme park.

After doing our favorite events, it was time to get something to eat. Our choice of restaurants was Diamond Jim's Western Show. There would be singing, cowboys and cowgirls, lots of laughs, and great food.

The food was OK for a place like that. The singing and dancing were very good, and there was lots of laughing. One of the showgirls, Lily, was very well endowed and dressed just as you would picture a western-type dancing girl: frilly petticoats and a very low, low-cut blouse. Toward the end of the show, she came off the stage, looking for an older, balding man. She approached one man toward the front of the stage, but he let her know he was not going to be part of her act! Unknown to me, Caroline, who was seated a bit back of me at our table, was making all kinds of signals to Lily.

So here comes Lily, sashaying my way! She not only swung her petticoats, she swung everything else! Then she sat on my lap! Wow!!! I think she said something, but I tried to act cool and not encourage her. But she wasn't done yet!

Lily got off my lap, stood in front of me, bent down, and taking my face in her hands, she planted a great big kiss on my forehead. She must have just put on a fresh coat of red, red lipstick before she came out looking for a receding hairline.

As Lily bent over me and planted that lingering kiss, guess what I saw? As I previously stated, Lily was very well endowed, and every bit of that "endowment" was within just a couple of inches of my eyes.

What was I supposed to do? Try to catch my eyeballs? Let them enjoy the view? (Oh, by the way, I noticed she also had an "inny.") Should I close my eyes? That sure was a fancy pink low-cut bra she was wearing. And she sure had a nice tan all the way down to that "inny". I'm not going to tell you how far my poor eyes had to suffer, being forced to travel all the way to...

Anyway, at the time, I was really trying to keep Caroline from seeing what was going on and trying to keep from turning red in the face. I never knew a strange woman could kiss so long! When she finally stood up straight, I decided to go along with her act. I rolled my eyes as if I was "in outer space."

You realize it was all for a few laughs. I really hadn't been affected by all that sort of thing.

Caroline and Lib thought it was hilarious. They persuaded me to leave that kiss on my forehead until we got back to the condo, so Bo could see what he had missed. Odd how some of the small children looked at me rather funny as we rode the tram back to the parking area. You should have seen some of the looks their mamas gave me. It appeared that they had never before seen a grown man with a great big set of red lips on his forehead, carrying his hat, in that hot Florida sunshine.

I'll never forget poor Lily. I guess she was just lonely and needed to express some emotion.

I'm still not sure what the proper thing to do should have been. But it sure was fun while I tried to make up my mind!

September 11, 2001

WHEN I SAW THE first World Trade Center report on my television screen, the first airplane had struck just one building. The newscaster said it was probably an accident.

As I watched the screen, another airplane flew towards the Twin Towers. But the airplane did not emerge from behind the buildings. Instead, there was the flash of the explosion as it hit the second tower. These images will stay in the minds of people all over the world, probably as long as they live.

At that time, my mind told me that this was a deliberate act of terrorism. Then reports came in about the origins of the flights, the facts that the airplanes were carrying full tanks of fuel, which would assure greater destruction.

At that time, I recalled a quotation from the Greek poet, Aeschylus, written over 2000 years ago. His words are as follows:

> So in the Libyan fable it is told,
> That once an Eagle, stricken with a dart, said
> When he saw the fashion of the shaft,
> "With our own feathers, not by others' hands,
> Are we now smitten."

It has been my privilege to use this quotation many times in my professional Boy Scout career when I presented the Eagle Award and Badge to a deserving Boy Scout. They, and all of us, must be aware and careful that our own words and actions do not become the "dart" of our own destruction.

The airplanes that were flown into the World Trade Center buildings in New York City on September 11, 2001, were our own commercial aircraft, loaded with our own aviation fuel, and were flown by foreign terrorists trained to fly those aircraft by our own citizens from our own country.

"With our own feathers, not by others' hands, are we now smitten."

More of Caroline's Humor

I MUST GIVE OUR daughter, Sharyn, credit for suggesting and contributing to the following. Even after Caroline went to be with her "Sweet Jesus" on December 7, 2000, our three children still remember their mother's quick wit and humor. This is not written in any way as disrespect. It is a way some of us grieve by recalling such memories, and I am grateful that our children have inherited the beauty of Caroline's humor by recalling incidences of our times together, such as the following. We all look to the time when we can share our individual styles of humor, collectively, with laughter and love in a place of joy, forever.

We checked Caroline into the hospital, June 25, 2000, for her "routine" mitral valve replacement. (Sharyn says it is routine only if it is not your own body being "routined". Inherited humor!) Caroline had already gone through many standard tests preparatory to this planned, needed surgery. (Preparatory standard procedures means running up the medical bills.) So after going through Admitting, she had the usual last-minute tests to be sure she would not contaminate the hospital. (Or, there is no room ready yet.) We were in a waiting room, and Caroline, being up to the occasion, again exhibited her sense of humor.

In this waiting room there were gathered most of the family. Behind the pulled curtain was our daughter Sharyn (her family was in Texas), son Rick and his wife Diane, and one of their four children, Christin, and daughter Nancy with one of her sons, Daniel. Of course, Caroline and I were there, too.

Inevitably, some discussion arose about my hospitalization in 1998. I started making comparisons to my "long, difficult, and almost fatal stay, about the conditions of the hospital, the nurses, food, etc., etc." That is when Caroline, in her sweet, gentle, loving, and surprisingly emphatic but humorous voice said:

"Dick, this is MY party, not yours!"

Do You Suppose?---Nah.

S NAKES ARE NOT MY favorite wildlife companions.

During my career with the Boy Scouts of America, serving the Thunderbird District in Lakeland, FL, I encountered both poisonous and non-poisonous snakes: rattlesnakes, copperhead, coral, black, and corn snakes, to name a few.

There are many tricks to ward off snakes. One is to stomp your foot on the ground, every other step, as you walk through the woods. It looks sort of silly, but it has proven to be pretty effective. Or you could do like I saw them doing on the Gold Coast of Africa during World War II (now called Ghana). The grass cutters swung their long scythes as the accompanying "band" played a variety of instruments to scare the snakes away. The instruments consisted of drums, stringed poles, and a few chants. And the ground beaters kept time with the drummers and symbols.

Perhaps it is well that we didn't use the stomping method one sunny October afternoon back in the early sixties. It was customary for the Boy Scouts of America to hold a spring and a fall Camporee. At these events, most of the troops gather together at a pre-selected area to learn skills, compete in many fun games, learn how to live in the outdoors, and pass tests toward their advancement in ranks, This particular Camporee was a "walk-in," where the boys and their leaders had to carry everything they needed for a whole weekend, into the Camporee area. They would have to carry tents, food, clothing, water — everything. No vehicles could go to the site, except in an emergency. One half a mile of walking, carrying everything.

A group of us had inspected the site very thoroughly a couple of weeks earlier. It had to meet safety requirements, naturally. We had to be sure it was "do-able" for all ages of the scouts and provided for the few handicapped campers.

This Camporee was held in central Florida, just south of Lakeland. We had selected a site on top of a phosphate mining overburden[1]. The landscape is dotted for miles around with these piles of earth as evidence of past years of mining. Over the decades they had become re-vegetated with grass, palmetto scrub, plants, and trees. And, as God has provided places for all types of His creatures, there were some small animals and SNAKES.

So came the day of the big event. The boys and leaders arrived at various times that Friday afternoon at a designated offloading field. When enough were ready to "walk in," they were led to the starting spot where some poles had been erected as an entrance,

Because I do not believe in asking anyone to do what I am not willing to do myself, guess who led this wonderful Thunderbird District over the trail? Eventually, about 350 boys and a couple hundred adult leaders of the B.S.A. walked that winding, uphill path, through the scrub palmetto, through the foot-high grass, over ancient stones and fallen logs, under the stunted week, and finally to the Camporee site itself. The sun was shining bright and warm on us.

Yes, the sun was shining, and God was smiling, on US.

We had gone about two-thirds of the way along the trail, with the adult Camporee Chief, a volunteer, and myself, the only paid Scouter, leading

---

1. An overburden is a small hill of earth that has been dug out so the miners could get to the phosphate underneath.

the way. We thought we were alert to any dangers, but suddenly someone yelled, "SNAKE!"

Everyone froze in their tracks! At a time like this, yours truly both froze in my tracks and broke out in a cold sweat! What a combination! We were about 30 feet ahead of the main group of campers. When I slowly turned around, I saw the first group pointing at a log that we had just passed. Very slowly I retraced my footsteps, well away from the log. Sure enough, there was a huge rattlesnake, sunning itself on a log. It was at least six feet long.

We had to do something about that snake, because it might not take too kindly to all those people invading its homeland. It is said that a rattler usually strikes the second person that passes by. It was not prudent at the time to ask this snake why. Besides, we didn't take time to take inventory as to who was first or second.

Very slowly we got past the lower end of the log and joined the main group. The snake had to be destroyed because it was on our main trail. And if we just scared it away, the whole camp would be pretty snake-shy. That may not be bad, but this was one snake we could do without. Fortunately, the rattler had not yet coiled to strike. I do not like snakes, but to whom do you think they turned, to clear the trail of this snake?

One of the troops had a long flagpole with their Troop Flag attached. I asked them to remove the flag, which they did. With this pole, and another normal-sized pole, I approached the snake.

I looked at the snake. He, or she, (I really wasn't interested about gender at that time) looked at me. Then I had a real bizarre thought! Wouldn't it be nice to have a six-foot rattlesnake skin to make into a belt, or some such trophy? I began to feel like the Great White Hunter, or Tarzan, or the leader of the Safari. I'm kidding! I was petrified! Scared! Nuts! Crazy! I had a wife and three kids at home!

Slowly, I approached Mr. (or Mrs.) Snake. For some reason, it just kept looking back at me. It did not coil. Its rattle started to make that scary noise, but maybe it thought that guy in short pants, high socks, a broad-brimmed hat, and wearing a neckerchief around his neck was too stupid to have a chance against this big, big rattler.

When I slowly — very slowly — got to within the length of the long flagpole, I put one end on the ground and put my foot against it, making it tense. Then I put as much pressure as I could on the pole without breaking it, aimed it just behind the head of the snake, and took a deep breath. Or maybe I wasn't breathing at all by then.

When I let go, that pole slammed down on the snake, pinning it to the ground. What a shot!

With the head pinned, I used the other pole to reinforce the first one. To my rescue came the other adults, who handed me a hatchet, with which I removed the head of Mr. Snake. Then we buried the head away from the trail, very deep. And the "walk-in" continued.

The snake was taken to the entrance of the Camporee to be used as a warning to all: be aware of snakes, and take precautions. My thoughts were also about saving that rattlesnake skin.

Later that evening, someone said the rattler had disappeared! Who would steal my snakeskin? We asked around, but no one had any idea what had happened to it. A real mystery.

Then I got to thinking: Do you suppose that big rattler had gone looking for its head?

Do you suppose?---Nah.

FORMATION FLYING

U NLESS YOU ARE 20 years old, wearing Silver Pilot Wings, and it is wartime, I would not advise you to try any of the following tactics.

While waiting to be sent overseas during World War II, some military-trained pilots were assigned to fly tracking missions here in the States. This meant either towing a target sleeve behind our airplane or flying a prescribed pattern over an area where ground troops and artillery units would track you, practicing their skills for shooting down enemy aircraft — hopefully not with live ammunition. Shoot at the sleeves, but not at the tracking planes, please.

There was one incident where we were towing a sleeve with a twin-engine medium bomber. The sleeve is supposed to be at a safe distance behind the aircraft, obviously, because they did not yet think we were expendable. Tell that to one artillery unit of what we called "cannon cockers". The first bursts of flak I ever saw were in FRONT of our plane. That gets your attention, especially since we were in Georgia, U-S-of-A!!!

Back to formation flying.

The tracking missions usually consisted of three air-planes. We had A-25s, or SB2Cs, known as Helldivers — a very stable, heavily powered low-wing monoplane built for dive-bombing. Its single engine was big, it responded to the controls quickly, and it sure could drop out of the sky fast.

It was a nice plane to fly, but it got boring as we flew over the practice area, making a set-pattern turn so we could go back over the practice area again. Then, into a turn and back over the practice area once again. Pass after pass. Perhaps exciting for the trainees on the ground, but boring, boring up in the air.

To help relieve this boredom, three of us pilots decided to practice our formation flying. Naturally, we were already flying formation. But could we trust each other enough to really tighten up our formation, thereby making a smaller target? Why not try!

Three of us requested this type of mission as often as possible. Flight Officer Marv Strauss, Second Lieutenant Bill Lyman, and I were the culprits in this story. We got proficient enough that we could actually tap wings with the lead plane. The normal configuration is to have one plane as leader, and he would have a wingman on each side of him. By closing in on the leader, and just a bit above him, it was possible to actually lightly tap the leader's wing tip.

Then, believe it or not, we got to the place where we could almost bring our wing tips fairly close to the canopy of the leader. There was a slight deterrent to this maneuver, however. If you got too close, your propeller could chew off the end of the leader's wing! That would have been rather unacceptable. We sure would have lost our license, and we were not paid enough to cover the body shop bill!

Sounds like fun? Or just crazy? Well, it did relieve the boredom. But we really learned how to fly formation. Part of this was learning to trust your leader and your wingmen. Very important when you are in the military.

Then one day, one of my friends was unable to fly, for a reason I do not remember. As a result, another pilot was scheduled in his place. He was a lot older than we were (probably about 25). We told him he could serve as the leader, thereby showing respect for the older generation.

Off we go to our assigned altitude and our designated area, with our new leader and with Marv on his left wing and me on the right. We flew at a respectable distance between each aircraft in normal formation flying. Pass over the tracking area, make a turn to the right, come back around over the area again, and make a turn to the right after so many seconds. Back and forth. Back and forth. Turn. Fly steady. Turn. Fly steady. Turn. Booorrring!!!

One or the other of us out on the wing positions looked at each other and decided to have a little fun. We slowly tightened our formation. The leader did not notice. So we came in a little closer. Because we did not want to cause any damage, we did not tap his wings, but closed in a little more. We got in almost as close as we dared when the leader must have either decided to change his concentration and hazard a little change of scenery, or maybe he happened to see the tip of my wing "in his face." His eyes bulged, and he snapped his head around to see where Marv was. Well, Marv had his wingtip "in his face" too!

Our leader reacted by doing what we call "dumping the stick." If you push the joystick of your plane forward, it depresses the elevators on the tail of your airplane. This makes you go down at a rate of speed depending on how quickly and with what force you push the stick. Our leader must have either been frightened to death or decided it was safer on the ground than sandwiched between two idiots trying to chew off the ends of his wings. He really did "dump the stick."

Fortunately, the mission was over about that time, so we went in for our own landings.

It was rumored among our small contingent of pilots that so-and-so would never fly with those two guys again. Lots of laughs and camaraderie. But we did learn how to fly tight formation — with trust and confidence.

I'll Never Tell

I N THE EARLY 1970s, our church, Carmel Presbyterian in Charlotte, NC, had a talent show for the congregation. It was open to anyone who thought they had a talent. And also to those who actually did have talent.

As a member of the committee, I knew what the program would be like. Our Director of Christian Education said we needed to have about three "spacers," or fill-in activities, to give a couple of minutes between some of the acts.

As a teenager, I had taken up playing the harmonica. I even played in a harmonica quartet while in high school. We four guys couldn't play very well, but we sure had a lot of nerve and made a lot of noise. So, owning at least three harmonicas, I came up with a plan to fill the needed moments between acts.

The theme of the show was patterned after the "Gong Show," which was a very popular television show at the time. It was to be a very non-serious talent show, and the participants knew they might be "gonged" at some time during their presentation. It would all be in fun. But the audience didn't know about when someone would be "gonged."

We had a very talented pianist, Rick Bean, who had many credits to his name, having played for many well-known artists. He agreed to help me pull off a few laughs. We would use a classical, a western, and a ragtime spacer.

The first "spacer" would be classical. As I came to the stage, Rick ran his fingers up and down those keys in beautiful, brief introductions to Beethoven, Bach, Tchaikovsky, Mozart, Grieg, Brahms, and Rachmaninoff. (Well, maybe I'm getting a little carried away here.) I wore a white shirt, vest, red bowtie, and wire-rimmed glasses. My harmonica was a classical chromatic four-octave M. Hohner that my parents gave me when I was about 12. It cost $12. They cost over $100 today!!!

My parents gave my older brother piano lessons, and my younger brother cornet lessons. I got the $12 harmonica and the chance to tell you this story.

Back to my story.

Placing my music on a stand at center stage, I started to blow into my harmonica. With a puzzled look at Rick and at my music, I reached out and turned my music right side up. That is always good for a chuckle or two. Time was about to run out, so Rick and I finally synchronized our act and almost got a toot out of the harmonica. We had arranged for the person with the gong to be sure to "gong" me at just that moment. So with dejected looks, Rick and I left the stage.

During the second interval, Rick came to the stage and started several quick renditions of well-known country songs as I mounted the stage dressed in a cowboy hat, neckerchief, blue jeans, western shirt, and a fake handlebar mustache. Behind me, I pulled one of those little toy horses with wheels. Real Western atmosphere.

This time, I carried my little pocket-size one-octave M. Hohner, just like all cowboys carry out on the range. Just as Rick and I were about to treat the audience to some great music, guess what? Yep, the gong gonged again, right on time! Great dejection again.

The last time our services were needed, Rick went to the piano and started some real nostalgic music from the 1890s. He sure tore up those keys as I entered the Fellowship Hall from the rear. This time, I was dressed in white slacks, white shoes, a bright red, white, yellow, and green-stripe plaid blazer, carrying a bamboo cane, my mustache again in place, waving a straw hat at the audience as I danced down the aisle. In my hand was my trusty Echo Harp M. Hohner harmonica, the three-octave "warbler" that would make the ladies swoon and make the men want to reach — back to my story.

So I danced to the stage and put the harmonica to my mouth. By now, the audience knew they were at last going to hear the talents of Rick and Dick. Not to disappoint them again, I put on my hat, smiled, took a deep breath, and — GONG!!!

For years after that talent show, people would come up to me and ask, "Can you really play a harmonica?" I'll never tell.

Caroline's Retirement Surprise

C AROLINE WORKED FOR THE American Red Cross for seventeen years. When she decided to stop working outside the home, it was a big decision, because she was not only loved by her co-workers, but she was also a storehouse of information. She had worked in several departments, through many, many changes in not only the physical facilities, but also changes in organization and procedures. She was loyal, honest, and cared about the ARC and her co-workers. However, she knew it was time to leave.

On March 1, 1990, Caroline was given a great farewell party at the ARC headquarters, many nice gifts, her certificate of service, hugs and kisses, and tears to show the love she so richly deserved. (I am prejudiced, but truthful.)

How could I give Caroline something special for her retirement?

March 1st was on a Friday. I had sent out invitations, pledging everyone to secrecy, to a party on the second of March, Saturday. These invitations went to our children — Sharyn and family in Plano, TX, Nancy and family in Aiken, SC, Rick and family in Ft. Mill, SC, my brother Hank and his wife Laurene, in Columbus, OH, Caroline's brothers, Norman and Carmer, and their wives Rosalie and Pat, in Wilmington, NC. Also, I had sent out at least thirty more invitations to friends, both local and out of town. In other words, these people were from all over the map! The trick was to get places for them to stay, eat, and stay out of sight until 6:30 on that Saturday night. And to not give the secret away!

In the meantime, I had arranged for food to be ready, decorations for the house, table cloths, balloons, paper plates, cups, plastic "silverware," etc. Our daughter Nancy, our daughter-in-love Diane, and our son Rick were to set out all of the "goodies," take care of decorating, and prepare for when I brought Caroline back to the house — and be sure there were no cars in the driveway or parked out front when I brought her home.

I was to take Caroline away from the house about 5:30 in the evening and would plan to return at 7:00. All of the arrangements and arrivals had to happen between those hours. How those kids must have scurried around. I had food and all sorts of things hidden in the attic, in the workshop, under beds. The kids had brought some things, too, like perishable foods.

In the meantime, I had told Caroline a couple of days earlier to pack a small bag. I was going to take her on a little "get-away" trip to celebrate her retirement and to enjoy the freedom of no schedule. We would go to one of the department stores so she could pick up a jacket that she had said she wanted. I told her she wouldn't need many clothes. (She could save room in her bag by leaving out her nightgown. I wonder why she giggled?)

Then I was going to take her to the Shun Lee Palace for a Chinese dinner, at her request. I agreed, telling her we had just about time for that. After we had eaten, it was about 6:40. We got in the car, and I asked her to reach in the map pouch on the back of the seat and get the tickets. She would then know our flight destination. She was surprised to hear that I had arranged some kind of flight and that we were going to go to some faraway place.

When Caroline reached in the map pouch, of course, there weren't any tickets there. She looked sort of concerned and a little shocked. That was my clue to not only look shocked, but to tell her to hang on! I must have left them on the table at the house! We would have to make a dash to the house, get the tickets, and hope we didn't miss the plane! I really did drive rather fast, and Caroline didn't even fuss at me for going so fast. I really played it to the point that she was convinced that I had forgotten the tickets. Up the driveway we drove. Not another car was in sight. As I opened the car door, Caroline said, "Bring my slippers from the shoe bag behind the middle bedroom door, please." Just what I needed! I dashed through the back door of the house, almost colliding with Nancy, who had gotten caught outside as we drove up the drive. I got in the house, saw that everyone had hidden in the bedrooms and the living room, then went back to the car and told Caroline that I couldn't find her slippers. She started to tell me again where they were, and then said, "Never mind, I'll go get them myself!" Wow! It was perfect!

Through the back door rushed Caroline, not even seeing Nancy hidden on the back porch, rushing headlong into the biggest surprise of her life!

It couldn't have been planned any better. Out of the bedrooms and living room, and it seemed from closets, under beds, the pantry, and who knows where else, came relatives, friends, and for all I know everyone on our Christmas card list. What a turn-out.

Our son Rick had rented a video camera, because daughter Sharyn was unable to come all the way from Texas. (She was included in a short section of film taken of a family photo.)

Guess what Caroline's first words were, as she tried to recover from the shock of all those people jumping out of the recesses of her home, shouting greetings and "SURPRISE"? She turned to me and said, "Dick Turner, I'm going to kill you." Had I ever pulled one over on her!!!

Well, I was never worried that Caroline would really carry out that threat. After all, it was recorded on videotape, and I used to delight in showing it to her. We have had many a laugh over the video of Caroline's surprise retirement party.

P.S. The next day, we really did take off and spent a couple of days in the Winston-Salem and Asheboro area. A wonderful, peaceful time of memory-building with the love of my life.

BUTTERFLIES

BUTTERFLIES AND HOLDING HANDS. The two go together because it was on our first vacation, all by ourselves, that the joy of both was experienced as if neither had ever existed before.

Just Caroline and me. By ourselves.

We were taking a trip to Annapolis, MD, Norwalk, CT, Providence, RI, Fall River, and Boston, MA. From there, we would go up through New Hampshire, over to Vermont, down to New Jersey to see a World War II flying buddy of mine, on to Washington, DC, to visit Caroline's cousin, then back home.

Enough of the travelogue.

After we had spent a couple of nights in Annapolis, we took off early in the morning and headed north towards New York City, which was "in our way" to Norwalk, our next stop. There was no way around it, so off we went.

As we left our friends in Annapolis, in the cool of that spring morning, I looked over at Caroline. We had been married for many years, were parents of three grown children, and were even grandparents. Caroline was the love of my life, but that morning she was the most beautiful person in the world.

Sure, I loved her. But there seemed to be a special need to touch Caroline. We may have been driving down a highway, but I needed to touch her.

So I reached over and took Caroline's hand in mine. I held her hand, resting on the center armrest. There was no reaction at first. Then she looked over at me.

It was a look that held a little bit of surprise, but it was also a look of the most endearing love that I ever saw. Here we were, grown adults, holding hands!

I was in love with Caroline, but suddenly I was in love all over again, in love with the girl I was in love with! Wow!!! That may not be good English, but I don't know any other way to say what I felt.

From that day until Caroline went to be with Jesus, we held hands every chance we got. (You just got "handed" a little extra story about my Caroline.)

But the title of this story is "Butterflies."

We had a very eventful trip, sightseeing and reminiscing with friends and relatives, seeing the beauties of New England in the spring of that year. We left the Boston area and headed for Franconia Notch in New Hampshire, in the White Mountains.

As we were going through the Kancamagus Pass, heading north, suddenly a cloud of butterflies passed right in front of our windshield. It was a huge mass of them.

They were Monarch butterflies, migrating from who knows where. How beautiful they were, and how they filled the air!

Caroline and I were amazed and thrilled to see so many at one time. This must have been the moment that Caroline fell in love with these creatures. From then on, she started collecting butterfly pins to wear on her shoulder. Seldom was she seen without a butterfly pin.

We were so blessed to have traveled to so many parts of the world. Everywhere we went, it became a requirement that we get Caroline a butterfly pin. Family and friends who traveled to places where we had not been brought Caroline a butterfly. She ended up with a collection of over 80 pins.

Caroline loved butterflies. They are the symbol of new life, and Caroline loved life.

When Caroline was called to "migrate" and be with the Lord, naturally, she left those butterfly pins behind. Members of our family selected the ones they wanted, and there were certain people who we knew would like to have a remembrance of Caroline's love. It was the beginning of the great migration of Caroline's butterflies.

I took the remainder of the collection to the church, and Caroline's friends took whichever pin or pins they desired. The love that Caroline had for others was being spread further and further. Each time I see one of those pins on the shoulder of one of the ladies of our church, I see the amazement on Caroline's face when we first saw that mass of Monarch butterflies in Kancamagus Pass.

My brothers, don't hesitate to reach over and take your wife's hand. Don't resist the need to touch. Encourage each other to speak words of love, and show the joy of walking hand in hand. Show the world that you are in love, every year that you are together. Be like the butterflies. Go to all the places you can, together. Share the Lord's love, and your life will be as beautiful as a butterfly.

One day, if the Lord is willing, I will be able to once again reach over and take Caroline's hand in mine. Once again, I will be able to touch the love of my life.

TEARS

APRIL 3, 2002

Every night I get on my knees
And talk to my God on high.
Thanking Him for my Caroline.
But to lose Caroline! Why?
And then I cry.

The many years that we had shared,
Fifty-six years and then some,
Soon all came flooding back to me.
Oh, how I felt so lonesome
And then I cried more.

No matter how long I do kneel,
While lifting up other prayers,
My loss keeps coming back to me,
Then even more my heart tears
And then I cry even more.

I know her days of suffering,
I know she had talked to God.

I know her faith was, oh, so strong,
She was ready for His nod
And the tears began to ebb.

This helps somewhat to ease the pain,
I focus then on this thought:
Caroline is now in heaven,
Her Spirit, Jesus had bought
And I wipe the tears away.

Caroline loved her Lord Jesus,
She praised Him in every way.
He was her guide in all she did,
"Sweet Jesus" I'd hear her say
And I cry some more.

The pain gets too hard to bear,
So I ask Jesus to aid me,
To tell me His promise true.
Then through the tears I see
Even though the tears still flow

By keeping faith that we some day
Will meet again, some time near.
That we will then reunite with
Those we love most and hold dear
ALWAYS.

So the tears flow,
but peace comes again.

What a Way to Learn to Fly!

I T HAD BEEN RAINING a lot in Arkansas back in April and May of 1944. We Aviation Cadets were looking forward to our graduation as flying officers in the Army Air Corps; regardless of the weather, we needed to get flying time in order to earn our Silver Wings. That meant we flew whenever there was a break in the rain. Not being experienced flyers, the instructors were very cautious about letting us fly. The runways were clear, but the ground beside the taxiways and landing strips was mud!!! "Just don't let your wheels go off the edges," we were told over and over.

Besides the main airfield, we used auxiliary training fields. They had makeshift control towers to keep some sort of order and to train us in discipline and etiquette. The day to which I now refer was clear, some crosswind, and was toward the end of our training in twin-engine aircraft. Our next step was to graduate and then be assigned to an overseas medium bomber unit.

My co-pilot, also a cadet finishing his training, and I had taken off, then flown to one of the auxiliary fields where I would practice touch-and-go landings. That means we would actually get permission to land, get in the landing pattern, and go in for a landing. The difference was that we would touch our wheels down on the runway; then we would advance the throttle to full power and take off before we lost too much speed. After we had enough speed to become airborne again, we flew a pattern to join the rest of the airplanes practicing the same touch-and-go pattern.

The one thing that you learn is that you need your flaps down when you are in the landing pattern, in order to be able to slow your speed, but maintain as much lift as possible. Otherwise, you may stall out. That is not acceptable. You may end up messing up the runway, bending propellers, breaking engines, and tearing up an airplane. And probably get killed in the crash. Totally unacceptable.

We had made one touch-and-go landing with no problem. On our second attempt, we got our "green light" to land. The two engines both checked out and were set for landing. The props were at maximum settings for the next take-off. The flaps were down. The gear was down and locked. We were in a slight "crab" because the wind had gotten much stronger (a "crab" means your airplane is aimed into the wind, but you are flying in another direction, like a crab walks sideways). The runway was directly ahead of us when a strong gust of wind hit us, driving us to the side of the runway!!! Guess what was just below us? MUD!

We were probably about thirty feet in the air when I gave the throttles everything: "[I] bent them over the firewall." The engines responded. The props were grabbing the air for as much thrust as possible. Maybe we could get more altitude and more thrust. I held the yoke back, keeping the plane just above the stalling speed.

Then something happened that almost made us lose all possibilities of getting our Silver Wings. You see, they wouldn't award them to dead cadets!

For some reason — I never asked why — my co-pilot pulled up our flaps.

How those engines screamed as I pushed the throttles of those two engines to maximum power. The prop-pitch setting made the props gasp for air. How much pressure could I keep on the control wheel to maintain altitude before the airplane would stall for lack of lift? Worst of all, the wind had moved us from over the runway and the mud and put us directly over a row of other airplanes lined up on a taxi strip where other aspiring cadets awaited their turn to taxi out for takeoff!!!

As I look back on my life, and the near-death experiences like this that I have had, I am convinced that the Lord had to have put His hand under our airplane and kept us airborne long enough to get us over and beyond that row of airplanes.

And He was forgiving enough that either the tower operator was preoccupied with some other problem, or decided the pilot of that airplane was either proficient enough in that emergency to know how to respond, or that the pilot should go someplace else to kill himself.

Either way, we learned a lot about flying that day. One was that my co-pilot should wait for directions, and the other was to keep your nose up. Either way, "Thank You, Lord".

William Tell's Son #2

PERHAPS YOU HAVE HEARD the story of the famous archer named William Tell. No, he did not compose the "William Tell Overture," which is a piece of music. This Mr. Tell shot arrows with a bow. For some reason that escapes my memory, he was ordered to shoot an apple off the top of his son's head. Back in those medieval days, they did some odd things, and I am sure this was not considered child abuse. But the story has a happy ending. Mr. Tell was able to shoot the apple off his son's head, and everyone lived happily ever after.

My story is a true story. It is about an event at a Boy Scout Camporee held by the Thunderbird District, Gulf Ridge Council, B.S.A. This happened back in the "medieval days" of 1963. At that time, I served as a District Scout Executive. I was in charge of a district consisting of over a thousand adult volunteer scout leaders and over a couple thousand Boy Scouts and Explorers. Back then, the Cub Scouts did not take part in the Camporees. Each spring and fall, we held one of these camping events.

At these Camporees, we promoted good outdoor living skills, learned sportsmanship, and, through competition, learned to live together and have a good time.

We also tried to have an event that would be instructive, exciting, and entertaining. The idea was to encourage boys to try new avenues of interest. At this particular Camporee, we had invited a local archery club to demonstrate the sport of archery.

The archers set up straw targets with the usual "bull's eyes." They shot at and burst balloons. The grand finale was to demonstrate the "shot of all shots", which was shooting an apple off of the head of some volunteer. Of course, no one got trampled in the rush to volunteer!

It was decided by the great group of volunteer scouters that if anyone was to be sacrificed, it should not be a valuable VOLUNTEER Scouter. They decide that, as long as this was to be my last Camporee as their Exec, who else should sit in front of that straw target with an apple on top of his head to, hopefully, have it shot off with an arrow, but me? After all, I was their fearless leader, dearly loved, friend to parents and boys, accepted and trusted for all those long years. How dare I leave the great Thunderbird District! (Having served the District for five years, longer than anyone before, I was taking my family to another assignment in Aiken, SC. Besides, my wife Caroline and I had already been presented the keys to the City of Lakeland, FL, as a going-away gift.) At last, I consented. Actually, I think I was coerced! All I could think was that I was being given a REAL "send-off."

It was rather nerve-wracking to sit there with an apple on top of my head. I watched the archer measure off thirty paces, reach in his quiver — that is a very good description of my body — and draw out an arrow. It is amazing how big and SHARP an arrowhead appears at a time like this. He put the arrow to the bowstring and flexed the bow a few times. Then he turned toward me. Briefly, he hesitated, and then, with a steely look in his eyes, aimed that huge, very sharp arrow at my head! I hoped it was a little ABOVE my head.

Mr. Archer (Tell) seemed to hesitate, quivered — there is that word again — and then lowered his bow. Whew! He seemed to relax a little and again assumed his stance. Here we go again! When he raised that bow, I knew it was time to make my peace with the Lord!

How I wished that I could tell Caroline once more that I loved her, for her to take good care of the children, to tell them of my love for them, and to mind their mother, to save their money, be careful to associate with the right people, and to brush their teeth regularly.

Then a funny thing happened. Mr. Archer relaxed again, put down his bow and arrow, and walked to where I was sitting, still with an apple on my head. He told me that he was a little nervous that day. He thought he would like to take one last practice shot. Well, if he insisted!!!

The archers brought out a mannequin torso, rigged with wire supports so it could be fastened to the face of the straw target. Of course, the apple was placed on top of its head.

One practice shot!

Back goes Mr. Archer (William Tell wannabe) to his stand, assumes that straight, upright stance, puts the arrow to the bowstring, pulls it way, way back, takes aim with those steely eyes, and lets that arrow fly!

Through the air that speeding arrow coursed, straight and true, striking its mark with a loud "thud." RIGHT BETWEEN THE EYES!!!

As was pre-arranged with Mr. Archer, I let out a loud yell and headed through the spectators and back to the center of camp! The people thought it was hilarious! What a show we had put on for the entertainment of that Camporee.

Now seriously, you don't really think I was crazy enough to be a substitute for William Tell's son, do you?

TWIN-ENGINE NIGHT SOLO

DURING WWII, AVIATION CADETS were classified for either single-engine or twin-engine pilot training prior to going on to flight training. We would become either fighter or bomber pilots. This classification continued all the way through the Pre-flight, Primary, and Basic schools. If we made it that far, we were then sent to the Advanced flight school for final training in single or multi-engine aircraft.

At each phase of training, there was the possibility of being "washed-out," or disqualified. The "wash-out" rate was extremely high. I must not have messed up too much, or gotten caught messing up, nor did I kill myself in the process, because I was classified to fly medium bombers. The Army Air Corps ordered me to report to Stuttgart, Arkansas, to see if I could learn to fly an airplane that had more than one engine, complete my training, and hopefully earn my Silver Wings.

After several hours of flight instruction, apparently, the instructors thought I had become proficient enough to fly the aircraft without an instructor. One day, they allowed me to fly solo, with another cadet as my co-pilot. What a thrill! I had, of course, soloed in single-engine aircraft, which is a thrill like no other. But now, I was in complete command of a much more complicated military aircraft, even if it was just a trainer aircraft.

Eventually, I logged enough hours of Advanced training, and it was time to fly and land a twin-engine plane at night. The instructors were very particular about their airplanes, especially at night. Although I had flown lots of hours by now, both day and night, I must admit that learning to land this type of plane was different. All the other planes I had flown had fixed landing gear.

These planes had retractable wheels.

Fortunately, as we learned in our training, there was an alarm system that let you know the gear was still retracted if you got too close to landing and had forgotten to lower the wheels. Practice, practice, practice. Landing after landing, especially at night. Then came my night solo.

My co-pilot and I took off. We were instructed to fly the landing pattern around the field and then come in for a landing. We ran over the checklist: fuel pumps, oil pressure, landing lights, flaps, prop settings, cowl flaps set, and then contacted the tower for permission to land. The tower gave me the green light, so down we started. I lined up with the runway, checked my altitude, and started my final approach. Nothing to it until — a screeching siren filled the cockpit!

What was wrong? On my solo night landing! If I did something wrong now, I would surely be "washed out" from the Cadet Corps!

Then I realized that the landing gear red light was blinking. The siren was the warning that it was a wise idea to land the airplane with wheels and roll to a stop. The instructors did not like to see fireworks coming from the bottom of an airplane, nor did they like bent propellers! Cadet pilots come and go, but airplanes cost too much to replace!

You can bet that we two so-called pilots activated the lever that lowered the landing gear really fast! Good fortune saved us cadets for another day (or night). We could go on to graduate and serve our country, wearing our prized Silver Wings.

Either we got away with that landing undetected, or the people in the tower figured that we had displayed such great skill in that bad situation that we could go on to become good pilots. They never mentioned it to us.

I now like to think that the Lord was watching over us, even then, as I made my first twin-engine night landing. Was that a siren screaming, or an angel trying to get my attention? I figure the angel already had its wings, and maybe it wanted to see what was in store for me when I received my Silver ones.

Rusting Away

I have a needlepoint plaque
Hanging on my wall,
Done by my daughter Nancy;
She designed it all.

"Old woodcarvers never die,
They just whittle away."
But with my new hip this is
What she had to say:

"Now I know that old pilots"
World War II — that's me;
"Turn into scrap metal."
But how could that be?

I have a metal left hip,
Gold crown on my tooth.
Perhaps she means my iron will.
But I'll tell the truth,

Carving wood was lots of fun;
Flying planes was, too.
But with all this scrap metal,
What am I to do?

Now if in time I don't rust,
Or corrode away
This former pilot, carver,
Will just fade away.

Perhaps I don't whittle today;
I walk, but why run?
This old scrap pile will still try
To laugh and have fun.

A challenge to a facetious remark from my daughter, Nancy T. Blaylock.

Our Pet Toad

N EVER DID I THINK it would be nice to share a tent

with a toad and three other guys

in the Assam Valley of India, during a war

along with ants, spiders, and roaches.

That is exactly what we four pilots did. It was during World War II, and the living quarters consisted of a concrete slab, over which they stretched a four-man, double-walled tent.

Inside the tent, we slept on real mahogany beds. We knew they were mahogany because the four posts were actually rough-hewn mahogany poles. The bed rails were made of the same thing, only not quite as heavy as the poles. Everything was held together with hemp lashings. The "springs" consisted of rope that was tied crosswise and end-to-end.

We were sort of protected from mosquitoes by netting that hung from the top rails, which helped make the whole arrangement fairly stable. That is, if you didn't toss too much when you got a chance to use the bed. In case a stray mosquito or two happened to get inside the netting, we, of course, were responsible for our own safety.

The military also took precautions in the event some of those mosquitoes carried the disease of choice in that part of the world: malaria. The precautions consisted of a daily ingestion of a yellow pill, called

Atabrin. Those pills turned your skin yellow. Yes, yellow. When we came back home, we were truly yellow! It took months for some of us to fade out enough to return to our natural color.

Those top rails also acted as a sort of shelf, on which we stored our personal B-4 bag, a duffel bag, and any other treasures we may have accumulated. This kept most of the crawling vermin out of our clothes and underwear. Our boots were sometimes home to snakes, so it was always good to keep them as far from the floor as possible. You never put your boots on without a full inspection.

The ants seemed to be most adventurous. They liked to travel up the bedposts, along the upper rail, and then back down the other side — if they didn't find some reason to stop for a picnic along the way. We learned really quickly not to leave anything edible around. Fortunately, the ants traveled outside the netting — most of the time.

Enough about the creepy-crawly and buzzing things. What about the toad?

In India, they have some rather large beetles and roaches. They sometimes took up residence inside our tent. Until we were visited by a quite large toad.

Did you know that a toad has a very, very long tongue? I have heard that it is sometimes as long as six feet. I have not done research on this, but I can tell you about our pet toad.

That toad was at least ten inches from nose to tail. Do toads have a tail? I never got a chance to check our pet, because when he (or she?) arrived each night, hopping onto the concrete slab by some unknown entry through the net wall of our tent, we just let Toad go to work.

That toad had the most patience of any living creature I ever knew. We watched Toad sit in one spot for what seemed like hours, waiting for a bug, beetle, or roach to venture into our sacred space. Or perhaps I should say It's sacred space. It sat perfectly still, waiting. It must have had hypnotic powers, because eventually, some kind of tasty morsel would not only creep onto our floor, it would actually sit and look at Toad for a period of time, and then creep into range of Toad's tongue.

Then the creepy-crawly thing would disappear. Toad's tongue was so fast you could never actually see it flick out and capture its next meal. That is, if you happened to blink your eye at the wrong time. It was fascinating to sit and watch this form of entertainment, which at times made us think we were losing our minds. They say war is hell. But not if you have a toad as a pet.

At least Toad helped keep the bugs under control, if not our minds. It was time to go home!!!

Hot Pilot – 23 Years Later

Our friends and acquaintances in Aiken, SC, were many and varied. I was serving as the District Scout Executive of the Yamasee District with the Boy Scouts of America in the Georgia-Carolina Council. The volunteer scouters were talented in many ways. One such friend, whose name is Don, had a side-by-side, single-engine Luscombe airplane.

He knew I had been a pilot in World War II, so one day he invited me to take a little spin with him. I had not flown an airplane since my release from active duty back in February of 1946. I really had shied away from flying in any private planes, being sort of superstitious after my last two missions overseas, and having concern for the feelings of my loving wife, Caroline. But time has a way of easing memories, so Caroline said to go ahead. She knew flying was still in my blood. I always look up at airplanes flying overhead.

Our son Rick would drive us to the small field outside of Aiken, where we would meet Don. Rick had never been up in an airplane, so Don took him for a short ride. After that, Rick drove back home. Don would take me home after our flight.

Don took off and into the wild blue yonder we flew. Shortly, Don asked me if I wanted to try my hand at flying again. Not to brag, but how easily and naturally it all came back to me. I tried some "S" turns, even a couple of stalls, to get the feel of the aircraft. I was flying again!

Don asked if I wanted to fly to Augusta, Georgia, land at Bush Field, and get a cup of coffee. I was doing the flying, so, using my great navigational skills, I set a course for Augusta.

Augusta was only 12 miles away. Those skills meant that I simply followed the Aiken-Augusta highway for about 10 miles — straight as an arrow — and as we approached the city, we could see the airfield. Pretty difficult navigation!

As we approached the landing strip, Don called the tower and got permission to land. I looked at the runway coming at us and said, "Don, you better take over. It's been 23 years since I landed any kind of plane." Don looked at me and said, "Go ahead, land it."

So, calling on the experiences of 72 1/2 combat missions (over 23 years ago), this old hot pilot lined up with the runway, eased back on the throttle, and very gently put that Luscombe on the ground.

A perfect three-point landing. Never even a slight tremor as we glided to the end of the strip and taxied over to the terminal. Boy, did my ego ever grow! Just think. Don must have been crazy to think I could land that plane. And I must have been even crazier to try it. However, if I had killed both of us, maybe no one would have known who was at the controls. But we were safely on the ground, and I set Don up for a cup of coffee.

Shortly after, we decided to make our flight legitimate. The Council Boy Scout Camp was near the airfield, so we thought we might as well go inspect it. This time, Don let me take off. Nothing to it, after that slick landing. Camp season was over, but perhaps someone should make sure everything was all right. Only the Camp Ranger would be there. After a few tree-top inspections, it seemed prudent to head back to Aiken. It was getting to be dusk.

The flight back was simple. Using our great navigation skills again, we followed the highway to Aiken and headed north to the airport. Again, I was at the controls, but Don knew that. He figured I could land the plane like I did before. However, a crosswind had kicked up at the field, and it was just before getting dark.

Down we go. I put the plane into a "crab" as we approached the runway. In this attitude[1], your plane is headed into the wind, but you are going straight to the runway. The Luscombe was a "tail dragger," meaning there are two wheels under the main fuselage, and a tail wheel at the back of the plane. The trick was to get the plane almost on the ground, take out the "crab" by using your feet on the pedals to straighten your direction, keep your wings level by correcting your ailerons with the wheel in your hand, and ease back on the throttle to control the rate of descent. If all of this is not done right, you can shear the wheels off the airplane. Airplanes do not land very well sideways.

Old hot pilot, after 23 years, remembered all of that, and once again put the plane on the ground — then back on the ground again — then back on the ground again — then at last on the ground once more. It was a good landing because any landing that you can walk away from is a good landing. Even if it took four landings in one.

The moral of this story is: when flying, you can not be a hot pilot. Flying will keep you humble. No matter how many times you make a lucky landing, it must not go to your head.

Actually, isn't that true all through life?

---

1. Attitude is fundamental aviation concept that directly determines flight path, speed, and altitude. Safe flying depends on knowing and controlling it precisely.

PILOT'S HALO

A s I RE-READ GENESIS 9:8-17, I count my blessings for many things.

Not only is my faith strengthened, it is fortified with words that come to us from ancient times, written by people who never knew what a pilot was, much less what a "pilot's halo" meant. In fact, it seems that not many people today know what it means when I talk about this.

Let me take you back to the days of 1944, when I was a brand-new pilot in the Army Air Corps.

It was wartime, and many of us were waiting to go overseas. Meanwhile, some of us kept up our skills by flying in light aircraft and training planes so the artillery troops on the ground could track us and practice their own skills. One day, I was up there in the wild blue yonder, bouncing off the tops of small cumulus clouds, flying the prescribed patterns, aware that there were some very large clouds approaching.

Storms were coming in, so I needed to abort the tracking session and get back to the airfield. As I started to turn back, I saw the sun shining through the clouds and forming a rainbow on the edge of the large approaching storm clouds. But this rainbow was different. Just about everyone has seen a rainbow that starts on the horizon, arches up into the sky, and then descends back to the horizon again.

This rainbow made a complete circle shining against the clouds. It was beautiful!

A rainbow in a complete circle!

When I told some others about what I had seen, they said I had indeed seen a sight that few ever see: a pilot's halo. At the time, I thought that was nice. I was one of the privileged few.

Now I will jump ahead in time to 1945.

When I was sent overseas, my assignment was to fly "The Hump." This was the affectionate name we used when referring to the Himalayan Mountains between India and China. That was the last assignment any of us wanted, because of the extremely bad flying conditions, and the casualty rate was about 25%.

(Caroline and I had only been married since October 8, 1944, and before going over to the CBI Theater, she informed me that we were going to be parents. But it was wartime, and we did what we had to do.)

On one of my missions, the weather was especially horrible. We were on instruments, but at least this mission was during daylight. I do not remember our cargo, but those storms just about threw us out of the sky. In those days, we did not have airplanes that could fly above the clouds. Nor did we have the kinds of instruments that could detect the storms over the highest mountains in the world.

Some of the mountains were higher than the altitudes we flew. Instrument navigation was the only way for us to hope to miss becoming a part of an aluminum-clad mountain, provided we weren't blown off course. Suddenly, we broke out of that huge storm and had an interval of open sky before slamming into another storm. It was then that I saw my second pilot's halo.

This time the rainbow was even more vivid than the one I had seen before. The colors were so bright.

The circle of the rainbow was bigger and more complete. But then I saw the greatest sight I have ever seen while flying.

The sun was behind us, but just in the right position to make a silhouette of my airplane right in the center of that beautiful, bright rainbow!

At the time of that experience, I wondered if perhaps it wasn't the shape of an airplane, with its wings out from the fuselage; but perhaps — it was the shape of the cross. Surely the Lord, even then, had to have gotten us through that storm and flown with me for the rest of my missions, so I could get back to my Caroline and our new daughter, Sharyn.

And now I know, as I get to know my Lord better, that He also let me come back to tell you about what I think is the real meaning of a Pilot's Halo.

God made a covenant with Noah, but it was meant for all of us. Not everyone will see a complete circle of a rainbow, but every time you see a rainbow, remember His covenant to all mankind. It takes two to fulfill a covenant.

The Hardest Day of My Life

MANY PEOPLE REMEMBER DECEMBER 7, 1941, as "the day that will live in infamy," as stated by President Franklin D. Roosevelt. It was the day the Japanese attacked Pearl Harbor in Hawaii, and World War II started for so many of us.

We who were alive on that date, and old enough to remember (I was 17), probably know exactly where we were and what we were doing on that Sunday. We remember the shock and indignity. How dare anyone do such a "sneaky" thing, killing AMERICANS, sinking our ships, and forcing us to go to war!

My parents, Henry and Ethel Turner, along with their three sons, Hank (Henry, Jr.), Dick (me), and Roger, were having a pre-holiday Sunday after-church dinner at the home of my Aunt Louise and Uncle Hugh Miller.

Dad was 40 years old — not concerned about being drafted into the military. Roger was only 14 — surely he would not be drafted. And the war would surely be over before he would be old enough. Hank would be 20 in January of 1942. He was in college, but a prime target for the draft, if physically qualified, and that he was. I would be 18 in March of 1942. As soon as I could, I joined the Army Air Corps.

December 7, 1941, became a very significant day in my life.

Then came December 7, 1945. On that day, the *M.S. Torrens*, a Norwegian cargo ship converted to a troop ship, with canvas racks five high to serve as bunks, arrived in New York Harbor. It was carrying many of us back home from India.

Fire boats were sending streams of water into the air from their hoses, people were on ferries singing "God Bless America" to us, and we were in the U.S.A. at last!

Not yet all the way home to Caroline and our daughter Sharyn, whom I had not seen, but I was on my way.

The next part of this story is very difficult to share with you. Not because it is a secret personal event, but it is very hurtful to re-live the hardest day of my life.

I will share my emotions and try not to flood the page with tears. The memories are with me every day of my life, and will be forever, I am sure.

Caroline and I were married for over 56 years. We met on August 26, 1944, and after a courtship of six weeks, we were married on October 8, 1944. Yes, six weeks!

On that day, Caroline became the permanent LOVE OF MY LIFE.

The night I met Caroline, I told Ted Drust, a fellow pilot, that I was going to marry Caroline. It was love at first sight. That may have been a blind date, but it opened my eyes to the most beautiful girl I had ever seen.

We had an active, exciting life. We were blessed with three wonderful children, eight grandchildren, one granddaughter-in-law, and in June of 2000, Caroline and I became great-grandparents. There is also a great-granddaughter, born in July of 2001 that Caroline never got to know in her earthly life. What a beautiful family!

Caroline knew she had a mitral valve insufficiency, which means that the valve was leaking too much blood into one part of her heart. Millions of people have this condition and live very active lives.

Caroline and I square danced for years, even dancing on top of Pike's Peak. We traveled to many parts of the world and enjoyed life. During the last couple of years, Caroline seemed to get out of breath quicker than before. She even climbed to the top of Mount Masada in Israel in 1999, in spite of this problem.

She loved life.

Finally, Caroline decided to have her heart valve repaired or replaced. Any surgery is serious, and none is routine. Especially to the patient.

Assured that it was a fairly common procedure, we went through with the surgery. All seemed to be normal, and we were expecting her to stay in the hospital for a week to ten days. She entered the hospital June 26, 2000.

The second day after the surgery, they sat Caroline in a bedside recovery chair. When I went into the Intensive Care Unit to see her that morning, Caroline said to me: "Dick, I have had a talk with God. He told me that He had changed His mind. I know my Jesus, and I am ready when He calls me. Be sure the children know that I am ready."

Wow!!! She was serious, very alert, and coherent.

So, in my great wisdom, I tried to assure Caroline that God had indeed changed His mind. He was going to let her get well and continue to serve her Lord, be a continuing inspiration for her family, travel, dance — but somehow, I do not think I ever came near to convincing her. She repeated her affirmation and request. I assured her that I would tell our children, which I did that morning.

What we did not know was that all had not gone well. Apparently, something had happened in surgery. The details are too hurtful to put in this story.

At 5:00 a.m. one morning, days after her heart surgery, I was called and asked to have the family come to the hospital. Caroline was not going to survive the day.

There was only one hope to save her: surgery that was not expected to be successful.

But the Lord pulled her through, after they removed four liters of blood from her abdominal cavity. More time in the ICU on respirators and all kinds of machines. Her internal organs had been damaged, and it was touch-and-go for weeks.

After a couple of months of fighting to stay alive, Caroline was finally able to be moved to the progressive care and then to the rehabilitation wing of the hospital. There she progressed to a wheelchair, and was even beginning to learn how to stand up with the help of therapists.

In November, Caroline was moved out of the hospital to a nursing facility that had a more specialized rehabilitation program. We were sure she was going to be able to come home, perhaps by Christmas.

About mid-November, Caroline complained of abdominal pains. She progressively lost her appetite. She and I both asked for a CT scan to determine her problem. But the doctor said Caroline did not have enough symptoms to justify it.

The day before Thanksgiving, our son Rick rented a van that had a lift. We were able to take Caroline to our home, where most all of our family had assembled. She even got to hold her first great-grandchild, Cameron Reid Larson, from Texas. We took Caroline back to the nursing facility for the night.

The next day, Thanksgiving, we all had dinner at a local restaurant. After dinner, we came back to our home again. Caroline was sort of tired, so we got her on our bed where she had a nice nap. She awoke looking very contented. I often wonder if she dreamed of her talk with God. How contented she seemed to be in her own bed again.

It was on November 30 that Caroline had a visitor that God had to have sent. Dawn Norman had been on the beach retreat back in the previous month of May that Caroline had helped lead. Dawn is a nurse.

When she saw Caroline, she knew she was in trouble. The staff doctor was called, and Caroline was taken by emergency ambulance to the hospital. It was there that a CT scan was performed, showing abscessed and erupted diverticulitis.

Emergency surgery was performed. After this surgery, Caroline was once again on life support systems. Her poor body had fought so long and hard.

On December 5, 2000, Caroline opened her eyes and looked into mine for the last time.

I am not sure what I saw in her eyes. The tubes would not allow her to talk.

It has haunted me ever since, until September 22, 2001. I now believe she was saying that she was going to be with her Jesus, that I needed to finally believe it, that she loved me, and was more concerned for me than for herself.

Then she closed her eyes.

My Caroline could not speak because of the respirator, nor could she breathe on her own. Her bodily functions were controlled by medication, and her heart was working via pacemaker and more medication. We were told, if she survived, her heart could only function about ten percent.

For two days, we (our three children, Sharyn, Rick, and Nancy, and I) were told that if Caroline did survive — which was unlikely — she would spend the rest of a short life on life support of some kind.

The children knew that Caroline and I had Living Wills, and we both had said many times that we would not want to live by artificial means. The children seemed to think it was time to let Caroline go to be with her Jesus. But, as her Health Care Power of Attorney, it had to be my decision.

After a very long night of prayer, the family met again with the various doctors, including Dr. Toni Stanley, who had done the emergency surgery on Caroline.

Finally, I made the decision that if Caroline was taken off the life support systems, she would be in the hands of God. This was not a copout. I believe that God can heal, even unto death. But if she were to live without those life-support systems, He would do the healing. Life and death are

God's decisions, not mine. So I agreed to give Caroline her freedom from pain and restriction.

At that time, Dr. Stanley reached out and took my hand, and the whole family joined hands as she had a beautiful, soothing, and uplifting prayer. Needless to say, she is our Sweetheart. I believe God directed Dr. Stanley to my side, as well as our family. Angels appear in all kinds of places.

That was the hardest decision I have ever made in my life.

I asked each member of the family if they wanted to go into the room to see Caroline, as she was — living because of the machines. They could say their goodbyes, or whatever they wanted to say, just in case she could hear. Tell of their love. It was doubtful that she could hear because of so much sedation.

And yes, I told her I loved her and quietly sang our song "Always" to her, as I had done at least once every day that she had been in the hospital. I hope she heard me.

It was time for the staff to do what they needed to do. We all left. The family had seen Caroline in her time of need. They saw all that support system.

Then I asked the family to come back into the room. There were no tubes, pumps, or noises of machines. Peaceful Caroline. The staff moved Caroline to a suite on another floor, where we could all be together.

She was asleep. Deep, beautiful sleep. She wasn't in pain, and she was in as deep a sleep as I have seen. In fact, Caroline even snored! This amused the kids. And me too, because I had slept with this beautiful woman for over 56 years, and always enjoyed the occasional little sounds of contentment as we snuggled together, reminding me of how fortunate I was to have my Caroline beside me. But for a short time, she was reminding all of us that she was still with us.

Caroline's breathing got slower and shallower. Finally, the LOVE OF MY LIFE, my beautiful Caroline, took one last breath and, with such a peaceful expression, went to be with her Jesus.

On her pillow was the music box that I had made for her several years ago. We had brought it so she could hear it while she was conscious over the past week. Of course, the tune that was playing was the one I sang to her — Always.

It was December 7, 2000, the hardest and most significant day of my life.

Scolded by a Little Red Bird

ON A BEAUTIFUL SPRING morning, March 26, 2001, I had just left the Men's Prayer Breakfast that had become part of my routine on Monday mornings since my wife Caroline had gone to be with the Lord the previous December 7, 2000.

That morning seemed to be filled with extra emotions, because so many memories flooded in on me. I was hurting more than usual, so I went over to the Columbarium, located on the grounds of Carmel Presbyterian Church, where we had been members for so many years.

In the center of this place of peace and quiet stands a large memorial that holds the names, on bronze plaques, of those members who have passed on, and whose remains are resting elsewhere. Family members may place the names of loved ones there, as a reminder of the love that is shared by this congregation, as a sort of "touch-stone," and as a place where we can get in touch with our feelings. I had purchased two spaces.

Caroline had been a part of the heritage of Carmel Church, having served as Circle Leader at various times, and always a part of the outreach of concern and love for the members when called. We participated in several Lay Renewal programs at other churches. Always willing.

Because the cemetery is much further away, this is a place that I often go to be alone with my memories of my Caroline. She is not in this garden, nor is she at the cemetery. Caroline is with Jesus, whom she loved dearly. But I still like the serenity of this place. I miss her so much, but her memory is here, where someday my plaque will join hers.

Beneath the budding trees of this quiet place, I went to the wall and touched Caroline's name on her plaque. Tears flowed in torrents. I was an emotional wreck!

I stood there bawling my eyes out when I suddenly became conscious of a bird up in one of the trees. It took a minute or two for me to finally locate her.

I knew she was a "her" bird, because she was up in that tree, looking down at me, and really telling me off! Even when I moved about in the garden, she kept scolding me!

When I finally found her location, she was a beautiful little red bird. Not a cardinal — she was too small. Besides, female cardinals are not as red as this bird. Very small. But how she could scold!

It seemed that after she realized she had my attention, she took one last look at me, spread her little wings, and took off from the limb of that tree. She flew out of the garden, over a rooftop, and disappeared.

Then it hit me!!!

Caroline was always so beautiful, especially in RED. It was her favorite dress color. Caroline was buried in a red suit.

God does not deal in coincidences. I was having a very rough emotional time on that beautiful, crisp spring morning. That little red bird was sent to me, like an angel from Caroline and God, to assure me about where my Caroline now was — with Jesus — telling me that all was well. It was okay to miss her, to love her, to let the tears flow.

Now go home and write about what I had just experienced with the little red bird.

This is what God said to write:

THE LITTLE RED BIRD

MARCH 26, 2001

I was in the garden crying over my loss.
Tears were overflowing, but then I saw the cross
That stood in the center of this place of such peace.
Even then I could not make my tears seem to cease.
I heard a little red bird up in a nearby tree.
Oh, how that little bird so loudly scolded me!
How dare I, in this quiet place, it seemed to say
Shed so many tears!!? Your Caroline is set free
To fly with the angels and romp with all her friends
Who are in heaven where their joy never ends.
That red bird scolded me, up in that nearby tree.
It seemed to say my tears might be shed just for me
It told me my dear wife was no longer in pain.
She can now walk and run.
But your tears can restrain
Your freedom, her desire; you on earth, her above
In heaven waiting to continue each other's love.
Then that little red bird up in the garden tree
Stopped all that scolding and, with a last look at me
Spread it's little red wings and flew swiftly away.

It had given me a message just for that day:
Thank God for Caroline, fifty-six years and more.
When you join her in heaven there is more love in store.
Now, that little red bird was an angel indeed
from my dear, sweet Caroline, that God has just freed.
she was so beautiful and so many, many ways.
you see, red was her color, and I will always love her
ALWAYS.

SOME DAYS NEED LOVE

APRIL 16, 2002

I don't know why I am led today
To come to this computer this way,
To sit and share my grief that seems
To fill my morning with broken dreams.

I want to share with my Caroline
More than we had, tho' life was so fine.
Our lives were full of such earthly love,
But now my thoughts are of her above.

Above, holding hands with her Jesus,
Enjoying her life that always was
Her earthly life's goal when she would say
"Sweet Jesus, be with me through this day."

How she believed in His love of her,
Love that I would not want to deter.
How she expressed her sure love of Him,
A love that she never let grow dim.

She has now gone to heaven above.
She can show Jesus all of that love.
Hand in hand with her Savior at last,
Praising Him with the Saints in her past.

So the grief that fills me on this day,
Is just love coming to me this way.
Caroline says, "Broken dreams — not true.
You're just lonely. Here is what to do.

"First, you must let Jesus dry your tears,
So that you can see when the cloud clears
From around your lonely, broken heart,
Earthly memories are just the start.

"We will someday share a better life.
One that is free from stress and from strife.
Jesus led me to this life so grand.
Someday we three will walk hand in hand."

The tears of grief that I shed this day,
That bring back memories in this way,
Are memories that come from above,
Memories that bring back all that love

To guide me in the way I must go,
To seek Caroline's "Sweet Jesus" so
I can someday join them up above.
And prove again that, Some Days Need Love.

SMILES

Sometimes we smile, just to hide the pain,
Especially from those we most love.
I guess we just want to protect them,
Like your hand is, warm inside your glove.

Sometimes we smile when there is no joy,
To hide disappointment in someone
When they have gone astray, but returned
Repentant, hurt, the battle won.

Many times my Caroline would smile,
Smile through those long months of her illness,
Struggle as she fought to do her best,
Hiding her pain and agonized stress.

But the smiles that fill my memories,
Are the smiles she spontaneously
Would flash at me, with eyes so bright,
Eyes full of love, and meant just for me.

Caroline's voice could smile, when she spoke
Of her "Sweet Jesus" at any time.
She really knew Him personally.
Her faith was absolute and sublime.

The smile that hurts, but heals even then,
Is the smile I saw, even as you died,
I know you saw our " Sweet Jesus" then,
But your smile was just for me — I cried.

Grieving – This Is My Way

G RIEF IS ONE OF the most personal emotions a person can ever experience. At least, it has been to me.

As I write and you read about this part of my life, I ask that you try to understand me. These are MY experiences: crying, laughing, running away — or trying to — keeping busy, sleeping, and napping; all the ways of trying to get through — not over — the loss of an emotional, spiritual, sensual, and yes, even a physical part of myself.

Yes, I want to get THROUGH my grief — not get over the memories and love that make up the emotional me. Yes, I want to get OVER the parts of the emotions that will not reflect the profound love I had and still have for my wife, Caroline.

When I lost Caroline, my wife of 56 years and two months, on December 7, 2000, I lost half of myself.

As I write this, it may be a way of dealing with my grief. You will find me being very personal at times. I make myself very vulnerable to your reactions. Your understanding of my feelings will help me express my total love for Caroline, and by sharing my love and emotions for her, I will show my love for you.

Yes, I have read lots of books and pamphlets about this subject, They may be helpful, but they only mirror what I personally am going through,

They give me a variety of possibilities of what may be ahead, But they are from someone else's experiences, not mine, I must deal day by day with my own emotions, my own grief,

So to selfishly help me, let me share my grief in a few laughs, happenings, remembrances, and, sometimes, definitions, Such as;

HOT FLASHES — Because of prostate cancer, I have gone through hormone therapy, and I have had my share of hot flashes, almost to the point of saying, "We girls" (Praise the Lord, the cancer is under control, Caroline helped me through that).

Grief comes like hot flashes; you never know when you will get hit. Looking at a picture of Caroline, turning over in bed and wanting to just touch her, or wanting to ask her where the table cloths are.

Or looking across the back yard at the trees we planted, the azaleas, the flower garden that Caroline loved to plant with violets, pansies, or other seasonal flowers.

This brings to mind how frustrated Caroline would get when, in the morning, she would go look at her flowerbed and exclaim, "What has happened to my flowers!" The slugs had nipped off all the blossoms overnight!

Sometimes, while reading or watching a TV show, there will be a romantic passage or scene. Soft kisses that become passionate. Even reading the romances in the Bible can bring back the memories that we shared for so long.

Oh, how little unexpected things trigger those thoughts and memories — just like hot flashes.

LAUGHTER — We used to laugh together over so many inconsequential things.

The handle would come off the rake or shovel. To me, it was fine because I didn't really like yard work. But Caroline would laugh at me! Accuse me of goofing off. Then we could both laugh.

Sometimes the garden hose got dropped, or aimed — accidentally: of course — and someone would get sprinkled. She always thought that was funny, except when — well, later we laughed as she got dried off!

Neither of us seemed to be able to get ice cubes from the ice maker without dropping at least one. Laughter.

How about one of us hiding the towel while the other was in the shower?

How I miss that little giggle and the real teary-eyed belly laughter from my Caroline.

SPIRITUAL — So much of my commitment to my Lord Jesus Christ comes because Caroline was there first. She never pushed. She just set the example of how I should get to know Him. She led by living her belief. Spiritual grief is healing grief.

From the time we were married, we never forgot our commitment to God and each other. Our vows were inviolate because of our love for each other. We became "one."

I look back and remember how Caroline practiced with a hypodermic syringe and needle on an orange. She followed the doctors' instructions, as she needed to give our daughter shots during her illness of several years. I know that as she was on her knees giving those shots, or on her knees beside the bathtub trying to reduce those 105-degree fevers, or caring for each of our children during any time of stress. Caroline was not there just for physical reasons; she was there talking to her "Sweet Jesus."

We raised our children in Christian fellowship and the church. Our family grew spiritually. I grew spiritually along with Caroline, and in our last years, we knew our Savior personally, together. We prayed together and worshiped together. So is it any wonder that grieving is in part spiritual?

I must continue to worship, pray, and live as if Caroline is still with me physically. Even though I can no longer sit in a sanctuary with her, hold her hand, sing hymns, or attend activities with her, I would not be honoring the memory of my wife if I stopped doing those things that our love built through the years. My spiritual grieving gives me assurance that we will be together and hold hands again.

SENSUAL — Now this is sort of difficult. I am not about to share our intimate love life with anyone. But part of grieving is facing the sensual aspects of your past life.

Whenever I see a man and woman kiss, it causes me grief. Caroline and I did have our moments. Hours. Days. Years. I have not kissed anyone's lips since my last kiss with Caroline at the moment I saw her take her last breath. I do not want to. My point is that sensual act causes so many memories of our lives together. I remember the times of sneaking up behind her, taking her in my arms, and planting a kiss like there would never be another. Or her coming over and giving me a smooch! Or vice versa.

Grief really comes when I roll over in bed and cannot touch the person who has shared our bed for well over half a century. It is a very empty feeling as I get off my knees and crawl into an empty bed. Even the new mattress that Caroline bought when I was in the hospital is more comfortable in the center than on the sides. We were two that were one.

Do not read this as some sort of lurid story. It is what grieving does. It tears me apart. But it also holds me together. Not in telling others about details, but in my sharing the parts of my grieving that keep me going, through another day, another night. I can still laugh, and I still enjoy being with our mutual friends. I love my memories. I face my memories.

I will not wallow in the depths of unspoken grief. I will not let grief overpower me. Even though I have many times of crying, of feeling so lost and lonely, almost fearful of the future, I refuse to crawl into a hidey-hole and become sick from grief — and then make others sick around me!

God has left me here for a reason, and I can hardly wait to find out why. I will face my grief and keep remembering everything I can about "The Love of My Life, My Caroline."

Now, if I may, let me preach a little. Not that I always do as I say, but I try.

1. FACE YOUR LOSS. Do this by simply asking for help. I found mine in my beliefs in my God.

2. CRY BUCKETS OF TEARS. Go ahead. Let them flow — or they will drown you! Let those tears bring back those wonderful memories. Don't hold them in. Share them with others; the tears and the memories.

3. COUNT YOUR BLESSINGS. Tears have a way of floating out blessings. Honestly, you have some. Think hard about that.

4. SHARE WITH OTHERS. Speak your loved one's name — out loud. What better way to show your love? Or do as I have done within these pages and in my first book, *Third Chance*, write about your life and experiences with your loved one. It has been a way for me to keep remembering everything I can about "The Love of My Life, My Caroline."

5. LEARN TO LAUGH AGAIN. King David fasted before the death of his first son by Bathsheba. But after the funeral, David broke his fast. (2 Samuel 15-23) May I draw a parallel to this about LAUGHTER? Go back to #1 above. Then learn to recall the happy times, the fun of sharing a life together, the shared humor, the joy of giggles, and roaring laughter.

Don't get over — get through your grief.

Jesus, Please Talk To Me

April 22, 2002

At times it gets so lonely now,
Sometimes it's so quiet, you see,
I need to hear a spoken word,
Jesus, won't You please talk to me?

Some say You do not talk out loud.
So I did not expect to hear
A voice that had a human sound,
Not even if I felt You near,

But when I found You as my source
Of strength and comfort when I'm weak,
I realized if I kept still,
Perhaps in time I'd hear You speak.

As time went by, and I sought You,
By prayer and reading of Your life,
I found I had Someone to share
My lonesomeness, even my strife.

The more I shared, and cried out loud,
The more I took that lonesome walk.
I called out to my Lord Jesus:
"Why won't You ever learn to talk?"

But when I thought there was no hope
Of Him ever speaking to me,
I thought of an alternative:
"Jesus, will You please walk with me?"

That is when I know I heard Him
Speak in a voice, so soft and kind.
Words that told me to keep seeking,
Obeying, serving, and to find

Ways to help those who walk my way,
Lonely, hurting from their own grief.
"Share with them all that you now know:
My words, My life, what you believe.

Then you will know, deep in your heart,
In your Spirit, too. And You see,
As we have walked in My true word
You have heard Me speak, just to thee."

THE MARKER

DECEMBER 7, 2001

By myself I sit in Freedom Park
Trying to dispel the gloom and dark
Memories of one year ago
When I had to see Caroline go.

I went out to the gravesite today
To change the season's flower display:
Color to celebrate Christ the King,
Seeking joy that He, to me, can bring.

Changed flowers o'er the body of clay;
It wasn't Caroline there today.
Just my tears from December seven,
Sure that now her soul is in heaven.

Reading the marker o'er where she lay,
At last I saw the meaning today
Caroline chose those words, I am sure,
To show her love - committed and pure.

Not only for our years here on earth,

But eternally, sure of its worth.

A true expression that never sways

Simply two words: TOGETHER ALWAYS

LIGHT

WHAT DOES LIGHT MEAN to you? But to be fair, maybe I'd better ask that question of myself first. The reason behind all of this is a teaching I heard about "Light in your life." This teaching was given in an adult Sunday School Class.

Think how it must have been without electricity. In fact, it is pretty hard for us today to even imagine ever being in a place without the expectancy that even if there is a power failure, soon we will be able to flip a switch and have instant light.

Most of the time, you cannot go out at night and be in absolute darkness. In my way of thinking, I think mankind is not prepared to handle a state of absolute darkness. Our ancestors had the light of day, light from the moon and stars at night, then light from a fire, and eventually light from the burning fat in a small vessel, or lamp. Over the years, man has developed many sources of artificial light to the point of not being able to live without it.

This is all very well. I have nothing against light or its availability. My whole purpose in this writing is to try to put myself, and you, in a frame of mind where you can imagine darkness.

Darkness is the absence of light.

The nearest I ever came to the state of darkness and its consequences was when I was a pilot, flying over the Himalayan Mountains during WWII.

The weather over the mountains caused the worst flying conditions ever encountered by man. Sometimes we could not get over the high peaks because of ice on our airplanes, or there would be tremendous up and down drafts. The monsoon rains and the hailstones in the upper reaches of the storms challenged the nerves and abilities of the pilots and the ingenuity of man to build machines to fly through such weather.

Being made into an old man at the age of 21 sometimes causes you to not remember such times. But then someone says something, or you hear a teaching like I did in this class. It triggers memories of those long-ago experiences. I now come back to — light.

We were flying through some real rough storms, trying to get our C-46, loaded with war supplies for our troops and bombs for our bombers, to Kunming, China. There is a lot of lightning in these storms. And sometimes the leading edges of our wings, propeller tips, windshields — anything that was an edge presenting itself to the electrical charges in the storm — were illuminated with St. Elmo's Fire[1]. This is an eerie green static discharge that stays with you for short periods of time. This gives some semblance of "light." But it is all temporary.

Inside the cockpit, we had the iridescent dials, and sometimes we would turn on our inside lighting system to prevent temporary blindness from the flashes of lightning.

On this particular mission, we had been through what we thought was the worst of the storms and were approaching China. The moon was not out, the clouds were way above us, and we were feeling safe at last, relieved to have survived another night over the mountains.

---

1. St. Elmo's Fire is a phenomenon caused when static electricity is generated by storm conditions.

It was then that I realized that we had just cut off our inside lights. There was no light from natural sources. No city lights shining below. Just darkness. It was absolutely dark above and below. Even the stars were hidden by the high clouds.

That is darkness.

However, I had a great sense of relief as I looked at my instrument panel. There was the stability I needed. There was light for me to focus on. Without those instruments, lighted with iridescent light, we would not have been able to keep the airplane in a flying attitude. Light. Stability.

The teaching brought home to me the need for light in our lives. We need it to keep focused, to be able to "fly right." Light, again, is the absence of darkness. Darkness, to me, is negative. It seems to be associated with wrong.

In the Bible, we are taught that "in the beginning there was light." Again, the Light of the world is Jesus. What more stability can you get than from your faith?

I now think that perhaps I didn't need lights that night. I had a guardian angel called "Iridescent."

WHY LIFE

The longer we live,
And time passes by,
We sometimes forget
About time and why

We are allowed more
Than others to live.
But stop to think, you
Have more time to give.

Give back to all those
Who gave love to you
Give back all that love,
And then some more, too.

So take time to think
Who loves you the most.
Who holds you up, and
About you will boast.

Parents, or a spouse,
A sibling or friend;
Someone who will stand
By you to the end.

God has His own plan
To let you live 'till
You show your true love.
Then you'll know the thrill

That someone has known
When they first loved you,
Because they have lived
'Till they loved you, too.

ANGELS ALL?

We never know when we may be called
To do a deed we never have done
Before, but some kind of inner urge
Makes us react instead of turn, run.

In your wildest dreams you never
Could imagine doing such a thing
As helping some stranger with a need.
Ah Ha! Does this with you a bell ring?

Have you helped change a tire on the road?
Or maybe stopped a runaway car?
Or helped an elderly person who
Has stretched himself just a bit too far?

Has someone appeared out of the blue
To help gather toys that have, somehow,
Been left behind, while some young flustered
Mom packs her car with kids, set to go?

Have YOU been there in a time of need?
Or has someone, to you yet unknown,
Done some deed that even saved your life,
An act of sacrifice freely shown,

And then just disappeared from your sight;
Never to be known for heroism?
Did GOD send that angel to save you,
Some angel that's known only by HIM?

Maybe you have done a similar act,
Somehow you have helped someone in need.
Not conscious of how you're reacting
Has been for them an ANGELIC DEED.

While walking in the park on July 4th, 2002, I saw a very young toddler race away from his mom, who was gathering her picnic blanket, hamper, and toys, apparently ready to take the toddler and his sister, about age three, home.

The little fellow headed for the rock-edged lake where there were some ducks and where his sister was standing. Realizing the boy was sort of unsteady on his feet, and the water was about two feet below the edge, I knew it was possible he could fall into the water. His sister was not old enough to properly react to this possible catastrophe.

I stopped beside the boy and waited until his mommy was able to take over. She graciously thanked me. As I walked on, I noticed a rubber ball the size of a grapefruit under the trees where this family had been. The mom noticed it, too. I told her I would go get it. In spite of my disability, I was able to climb the slight hill, retrieve the ball, and return it to the mother.

I tell this story, not because my life is angelic, but when I got home, the Lord put it in my mind to put the poem above on paper. I think He wanted me to let other people know that there are angels all around.

Perhaps the angels get too busy sometimes trying to take care of people like me, so God uses ordinary people like you and me to teach us that we should not hesitate to be a "good Samaritan." We may never know when we are someone else's angel. Even me!

TALENTS

JULY 14, 2002

If I have any talents,
Please do not give thanks to me.
But if you think that you must,
First give God all the glory.

He is the talent, you see.
He first gave the gift to me.
Then He can bless all of us
With those talents that are free.

Think of all the talents that
Give witness all the year 'round.
All kinds of people provide
Beauty and words so profound.

Talents for all the great arts,
Music, teaching and so much,
Building, healing, witnessing.
But we must be free for such

Gifts to be manifested
Through our God who is above,
Free to be used, free to give,
Free to share His gift of love.

So look not at my talent,
Look to Jesus who lets me
Use His talent just for you.
He has truly set me free.

Then I can honestly say
Thank you, my Father above,
I thank you my Christ Jesus,
And Holy Spirit for LOVE.

REVELATION ---AT LAST

CAROLINE AND I HAD a very beautiful, close love affair for over 56 years.

When we were married, she said that her Daddy had spoiled her for 21 years and that I could spoil her for the rest of her life. Sort of one of those little things lovers say, in a kind of kidding, teasing way. Of course, I took her very seriously.

I had fallen in love with her the moment I met her on our first date — that blind date on August 26, 1944. So, Yes, Ma'am! And I must tell her I loved her at least three times a day. Yes, Ma'am! I loved my Caroline so much that there wasn't anything I would not do for her.

For the rest of her life, I tried to fulfill those stipulations. Not because she expected me to, but because I wanted to. No, Caroline wasn't spoiled in the sense that you see in children. I tried to spoil her with my love. As far as proclamations of love, well, we managed to live up to that pretty well, too. In fact, we didn't put a limit on that.

As a result of our commitment to each other, our love was strong enough that, even in those lean years of material needs, years of medical hardships with our children, career changes, and loss of parents, we always made it through. We never missed a meal. We were always clothed adequately, and we were always blessed with friends and family. Caroline took care of her own family by her example and her deep faith in Jesus.

Perhaps you can understand why I never believed that Caroline could ever love me as much as I loved her.

On September 21, 2001, I went to bed about 11:00 p.m. and eventually went to sleep. About 12:20 a.m. on September 22, 2001, I was suddenly awakened by the word "REVELATION."

No, I did not hear a voice. Neither was I tossed out of bed. It was just the word that somehow caused me to become conscious.

Then the words of explanation started to come to me. How could I possibly remember what those words were? So I jumped out of bed and got some paper and a pencil. This story is what was revealed to me that early morning.

"Caroline did love you, and it was an equal love. Think of the times she would reach over and touch your arm as you drove down the highway on your many trips together, and say, 'I love you, Dick.' Or, all snuggled up in bed, she would raise her head and let you know she wanted that one last kiss before going to sleep. Think about those three beautiful children she shared with you, their loving spouses, eight grandchildren, and one granddaughter-in-law. There are even great-grandchildren who are a legacy of your love for each other."

What a revelation! Yes, Caroline did have an equal love for me.

Then the message went on. Usually, the husband in a marriage passes away first. As Caroline so often told me, "Not always. Only God knows when and who will go first." Sometimes she would look at me and remind me that I better be ready!

When the Lord brought me back from the edge of heaven on March 8, 1998, I thought it was so I could tell Caroline I was going to be with the Lord in that beautiful white area, from which I had come. She must not grieve long and should try to get on with her life. She would be all right. Wrong!

The day after Caroline's heart surgery, June 28, 2000, she was sitting up in a big ICU chair when I got to see her. Caroline said to me, " Dick, you must tell the children that I have talked with God, and He told me He had changed His mind. I am ready to be with Jesus, so there is not to be any concern about that. But you must prepare them and tell them about this."

None of us really thought that it meant that Caroline would not come through her surgery. So, in our great wisdom, we tried to convince Caroline that God meant He was not going to take her at this time. But God did indeed take Caroline to be with Him on December 7, 2000. And I know that Caroline is with Jesus, completely well and full of her usual joy and happiness.

My life is but half a life. I am not asking for sympathy. I try not to feel sorry for myself. But I am extremely sad and lonesome for my Caroline.

If our love were equal, Caroline would be in the same emotional state that I am. Now I know why God brought me back. Neither He nor I would want to take away from Caroline what seems to be lacking in my life.

God loves Caroline more than I ever could, and I love her so much that I am happy that she went to be with the Lord before I did, so she can have happiness untold as promised by our Lord. She is so happy that she won't need me to "spoil" her anymore.

I miss Caroline, but thank you, Lord, for the REVELATION ---at last.

Thank You, Dear Reader

As you read through this book, perhaps you saw the author as I would like to be seen — as just another human being that has taken the time to share more of the events of his life with his family, by putting a record of these events on paper.

In my first book, *Third Chance*, I had the help of my wife, Caroline. It was a sort of spiritual autobiography, which made me vulnerable to this exposure of who I am. This time, I do not have Caroline to edit, re-write, correct my memory, and generally keep me focused. I miss my Caroline, the love of my life. So this book is the second half of our story, by the half of the person left behind to tell it.

My thanks go out to all of our children, especially Sharyn, who edited, corrected, and spent hours and hours via e-mail and telephone, encouraging me to give the family more stories of our "link to history." Thank you, Kids.

But it will be you readers who will determine whether these stories of events in our lives will encourage some of you to do the same for your family. (We all have different talents that are discovered, sometimes, accidentally. You, too, may be a teller of stories or a poet. You may want to re-read the poem *Talents* that precedes this.) I must admit it is trying at times to put a book together, but there is no earlier time than now to jot down notes, share experiences with your children, and family. Some call it "journaling."

My life, shared with Caroline, has been a life of goals, successes, failures, excitement, changes, laughs, tears, and a complete range of emotions. Just like most of you readers. And like all of you, the strength to get through this life depends on your faith and the commitment and love you are willing to give.

If you have read through to this last page, I again want to thank you for letting me share my life with you in written form. I would ask one thing: Love one another. ALWAYS.

ABOUT

*Lt. Richard W. Turner, US Army Air
Corps, 1944*

Richard W. Turner, Sr. (1924-2004) was a World War II veteran, decorated pilot, artist, author, and devoted husband and father whose life was marked by service, creativity, humility, and deep faith.

Born in Johnson City, New York, Turner answered the call of duty, serving with distinction in the China-Burma-India (CBI) Theater. As a pilot, he flew 72 1/2 missions over the treacherous Himalayan supply route known as "The Hump", an experience that shaped his character and perspective for the rest of his life.

After the war, Turner became a leader in the Boy Scouts of America, raised a family, was active in his church, and enjoyed painting, nature, and whittling woodcarvings. He shared 56 years with the love of his life, Caroline, and began writing in his later years to reflect on his life's most defining moments.

ALSO BY

Third Chance

Third Chance An inspiring memoir chronicling a near-death experience and spiritual awakenings. With heartfelt gratitude, he shares the faith, friendships, and miracles that shaped his life and restored his purpose. This memoir honors the love of his life, Caroline, and the encouragement and support of his family and community.

Stories from the Hump

Stories from The Hump A vivid and moving collection of wartime memories. The stories from Turner's service as a US Army Air Corps C-46 pilot flying over the Himalayas blend danger, humor, and the unseen hand of God. Turner captures the courage and faith of those brave airmen who flew The Hump in the China-Burma-India Theater of WWII.

www.ingramcontent.com/pod-product-compliance
Lightning Source LLC
Chambersburg PA
CBHW021152130626
46554CB00005B/1781